PLANES

for Stella and Egon

"Make your life a dream, and your dream a reality."
— Antoine de Saint-Exupéry —

PLANES

FROM THE WRIGHT BROTHERS TO THE SUPERSONIC JET

Jan Van der Veken

PRESTEL

Munich · London · New York

CONTENTS

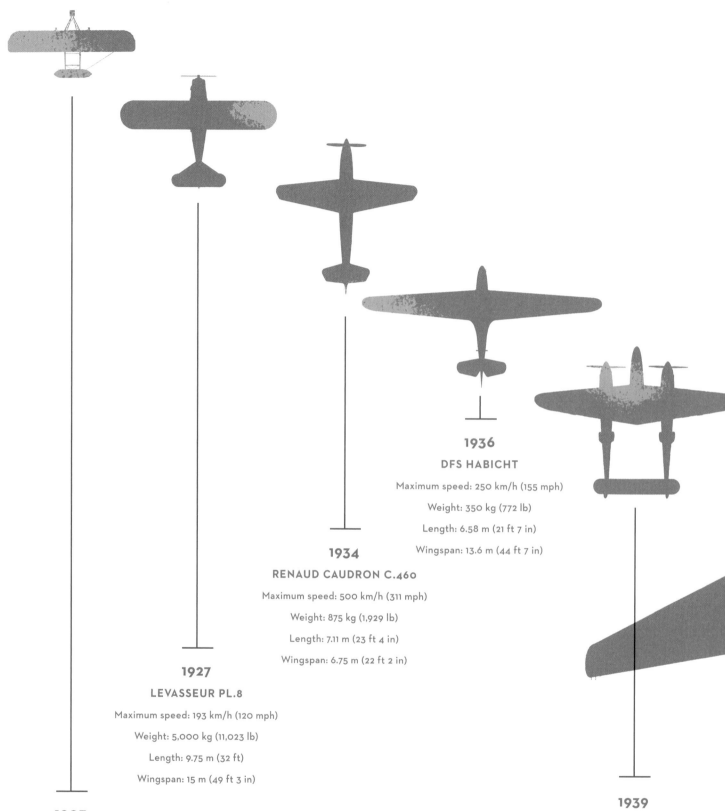

1936

DFS HABICHT

Maximum speed: 250 km/h (155 mph)

Weight: 350 kg (772 lb)

Length: 6.58 m (21 ft 7 in)

Wingspan: 13.6 m (44 ft 7 in)

1934

RENAUD CAUDRON C.460

Maximum speed: 500 km/h (311 mph)

Weight: 875 kg (1,929 lb)

Length: 7.11 m (23 ft 4 in)

Wingspan: 6.75 m (22 ft 2 in)

1927

LEVASSEUR PL.8

Maximum speed: 193 km/h (120 mph)

Weight: 5,000 kg (11,023 lb)

Length: 9.75 m (32 ft)

Wingspan: 15 m (49 ft 3 in)

1903

WRIGHT FLYER

Maximum speed: 48 km/h (30 mph)

Weight: 274 kg (605 lb)

Length: 6.43 m (21 ft 1 in)

Wingspan: 12 m (40 ft 4 in)

1939

LOCKHEED P-38

Maximum speed: 666 km/h (414 mph)

Weight: 7,938 kg (17,500 lb)

Length: 11.53 m (37 ft 10 in)

Wingspan: 15.85 m (52 ft)

1966

NORTHROP HL-10

Maximum speed: 1,976 km/h

(1,228 mph, 549 m/s)

Weight: 2,722 kg (6,000 lb)

Length: 6.45 m (21 ft 2 in)

Wingspan: 4.15 m (13 ft 7 in)

1946

NORTHROP YB-35

m speed: 632 km/h (393 mph)

ght: 81,647 kg (180,000 lb)

ength: 16.2 m (53 ft 1 in)

ingspan: 52.4 m (172 ft)

1960

PIPER ARCHER P-28

Maximum speed: 230 km/h (143 mph)

Weight: 975 kg (2,150 lb)

Length: 7.16 m (23 ft 6 in)

Wingspan: 9.2 m (30 ft 2 in)

1959

NORTH AMERICAN X-15

Maximum speed: 7,274 km/h

(4,520 mph, 2,021 m/s)

Weight: 15,422 kg (34,000 lb)

Length: 15.45 m (50 ft 9 in)

Wingspan: 6.8 m (22 ft 4 in)

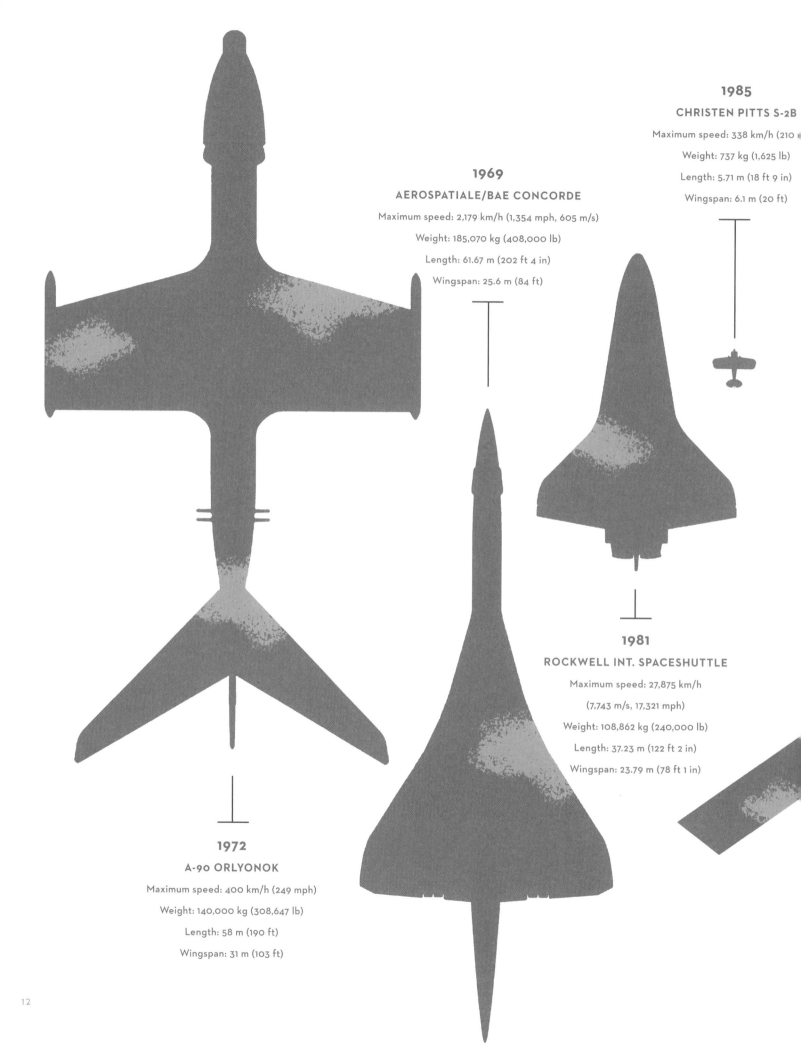

1985
CHRISTEN PITTS S-2B

Maximum speed: 338 km/h (210
Weight: 737 kg (1,625 lb)
Length: 5.71 m (18 ft 9 in)
Wingspan: 6.1 m (20 ft)

1969
AEROSPATIALE/BAE CONCORDE

Maximum speed: 2,179 km/h (1,354 mph, 605 m/s)
Weight: 185,070 kg (408,000 lb)
Length: 61.67 m (202 ft 4 in)
Wingspan: 25.6 m (84 ft)

1981
ROCKWELL INT. SPACESHUTTLE

Maximum speed: 27,875 km/h
(7,743 m/s, 17,321 mph)
Weight: 108,862 kg (240,000 lb)
Length: 37.23 m (122 ft 2 in)
Wingspan: 23.79 m (78 ft 1 in)

1972
A-90 ORLYONOK

Maximum speed: 400 km/h (249 mph)
Weight: 140,000 kg (308,647 lb)
Length: 58 m (190 ft)
Wingspan: 31 m (103 ft)

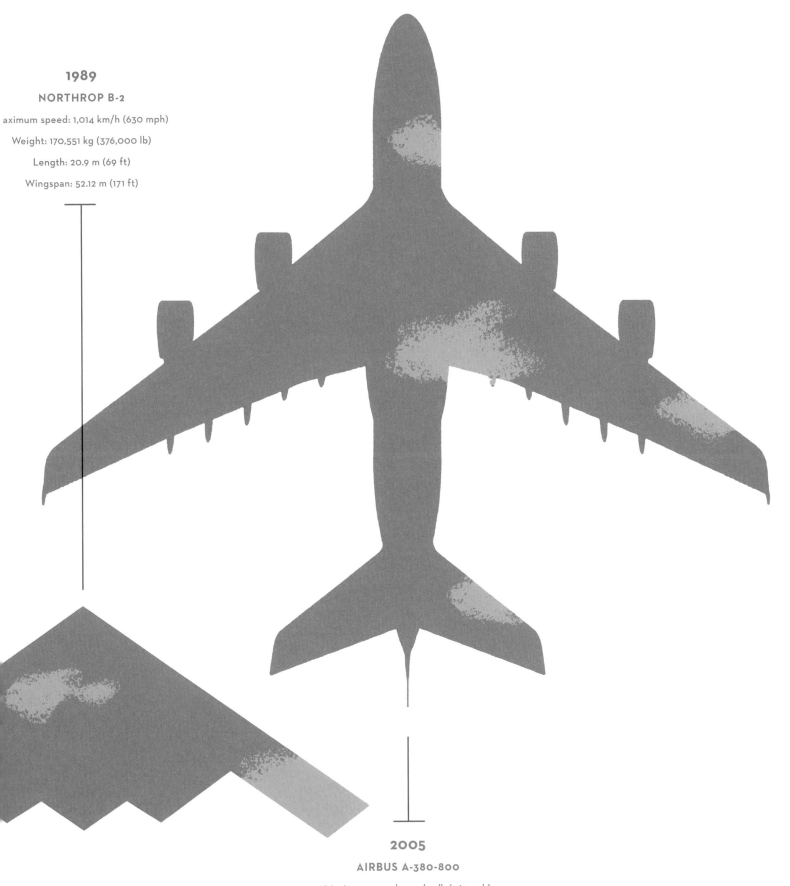

1989

NORTHROP B-2

aximum speed: 1,014 km/h (630 mph)

Weight: 170,551 kg (376,000 lb)

Length: 20.9 m (69 ft)

Wingspan: 52.12 m (171 ft)

2005

AIRBUS A-380-800

Maximum speed: 903 km/h (561 mph)

Weight: 575,000 kg (1,267,658 lb)

Length: 72.72 m (238 ft 7 in)

Wingspan: 79.75 m (261 ft 8 in)

AIRPLANE DESIGN

HOW AN AIRPLANE LOOKS AND WHY

PARTS OF A PROPELLER AIRPLANE

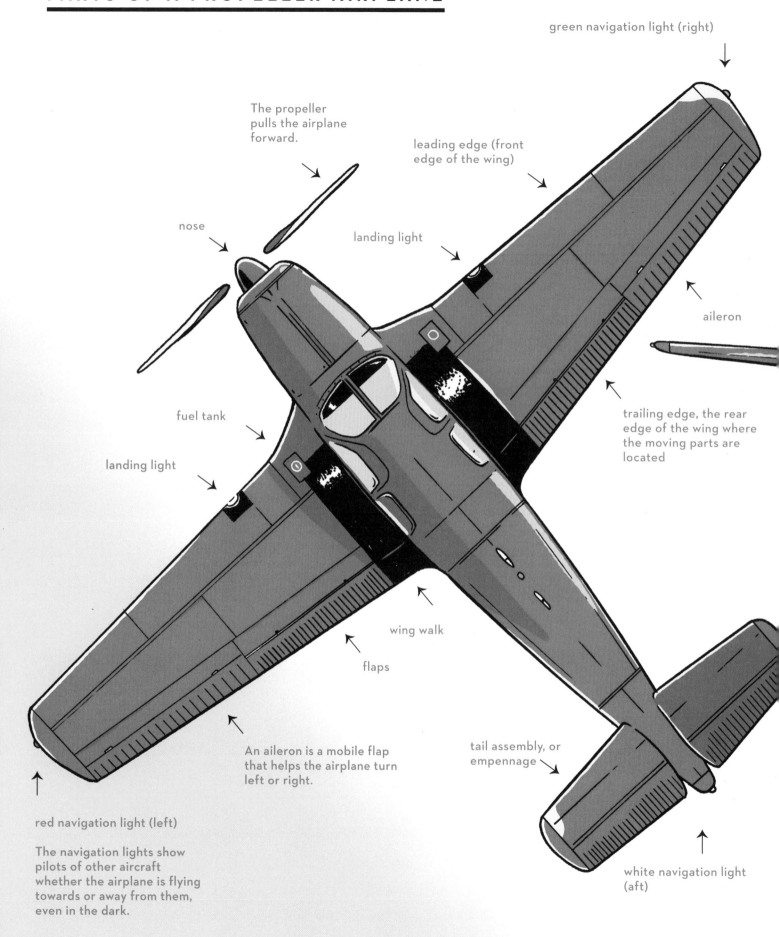

green navigation light (right)

The propeller pulls the airplane forward.

leading edge (front edge of the wing)

nose

landing light

aileron

fuel tank

trailing edge, the rear edge of the wing where the moving parts are located

landing light

wing walk

flaps

An aileron is a mobile flap that helps the airplane turn left or right.

tail assembly, or empennage

red navigation light (left)

white navigation light (aft)

The navigation lights show pilots of other aircraft whether the airplane is flying towards or away from them, even in the dark.

The top surface of the wing is curved so that the air has farther to travel than it does on the bottom surface. This lowers the pressure above the wing and helps generate lift.

The rudder and elevator help to control the direction of the plane.

landing light

landing light

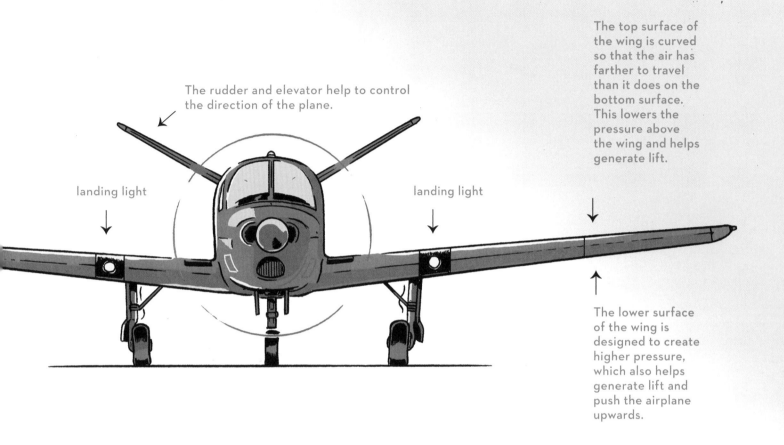

The lower surface of the wing is designed to create higher pressure, which also helps generate lift and push the airplane upwards.

cockpit

radio antenna

Emergency Location Transmitter (ELT)

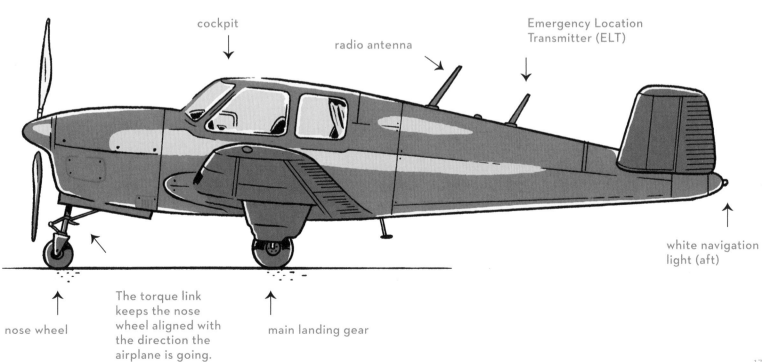

white navigation light (aft)

nose wheel

The torque link keeps the nose wheel aligned with the direction the airplane is going.

main landing gear

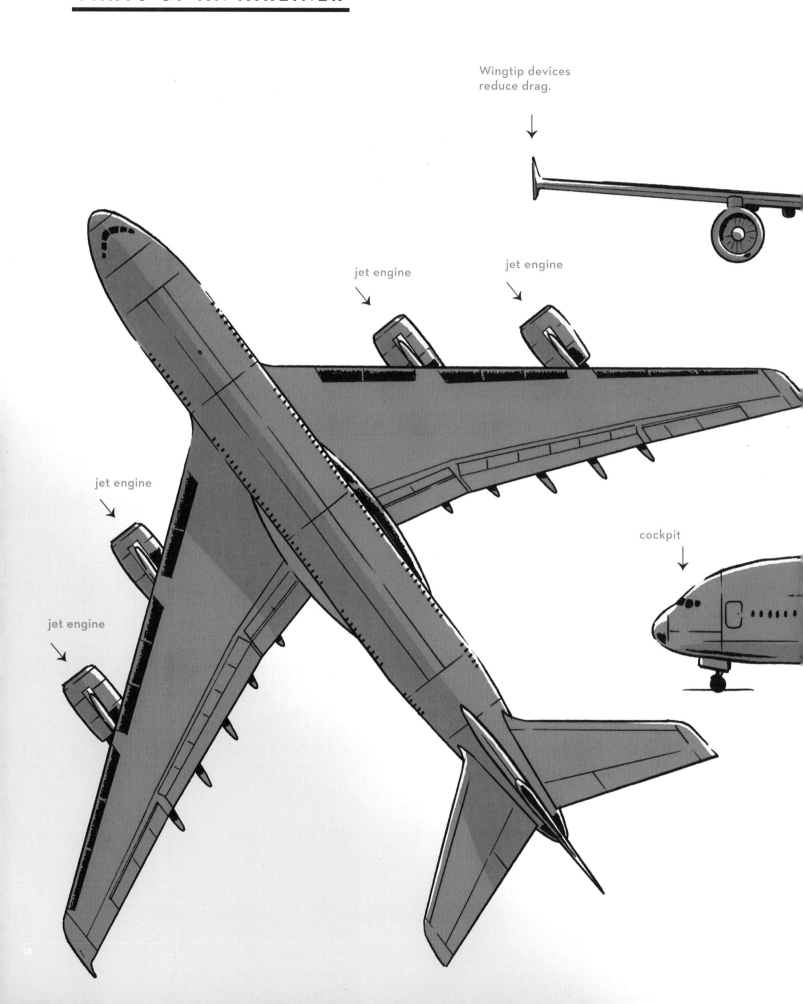

Wingtip devices
reduce drag.

jet engine

jet engine

jet engine

jet engine

cockpit

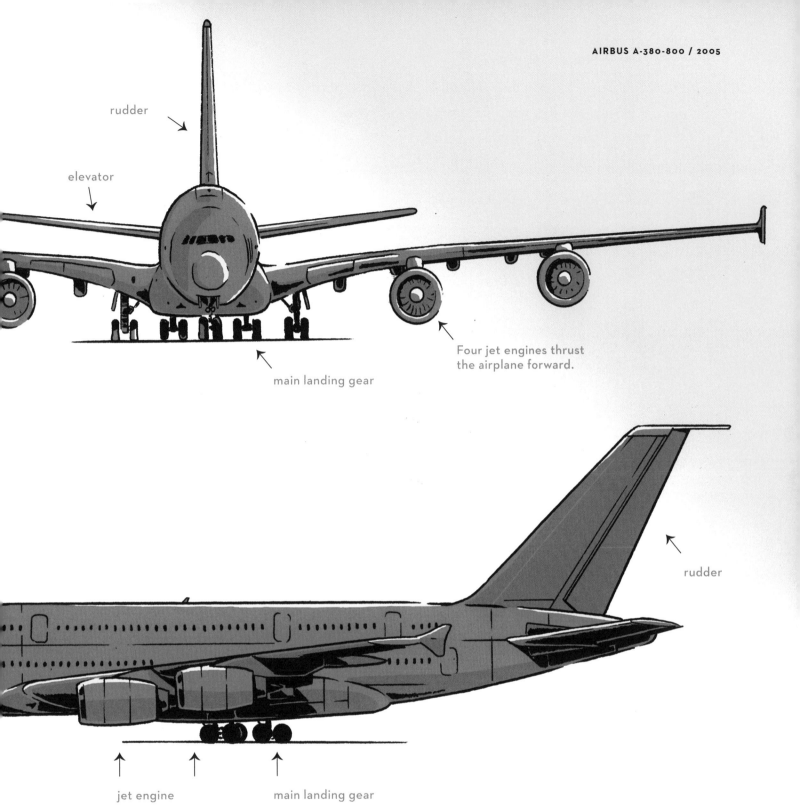

rudder

elevator

main landing gear

Four jet engines thrust
the airplane forward.

rudder

jet engine   main landing gear

WHAT FORCES ACT ON AN AIRPLANE?

To understand more clearly which parts are important in airplane design, we need to know about the natural forces that act on any airplane. There are four main forces. Some of them make it easier to fly; others make it harder. Gravity and air resistance make flying more difficult. An airplane is a heavy machine with a large mass. Gravity pulls it towards the Earth. Every aircraft meets with air resistance (or drag) on the wings, tail, nose, and main body (or fuse-lage). The amount of drag is determined by an aircraft's shape. Designers try to make airplanes as streamlined as possible. When they succeed, the plane cuts through the air at high speed, meeting the least possible resistance. The forces that make flight easier come from the engine and the wings. The engine turns a propeller and generates thrust,

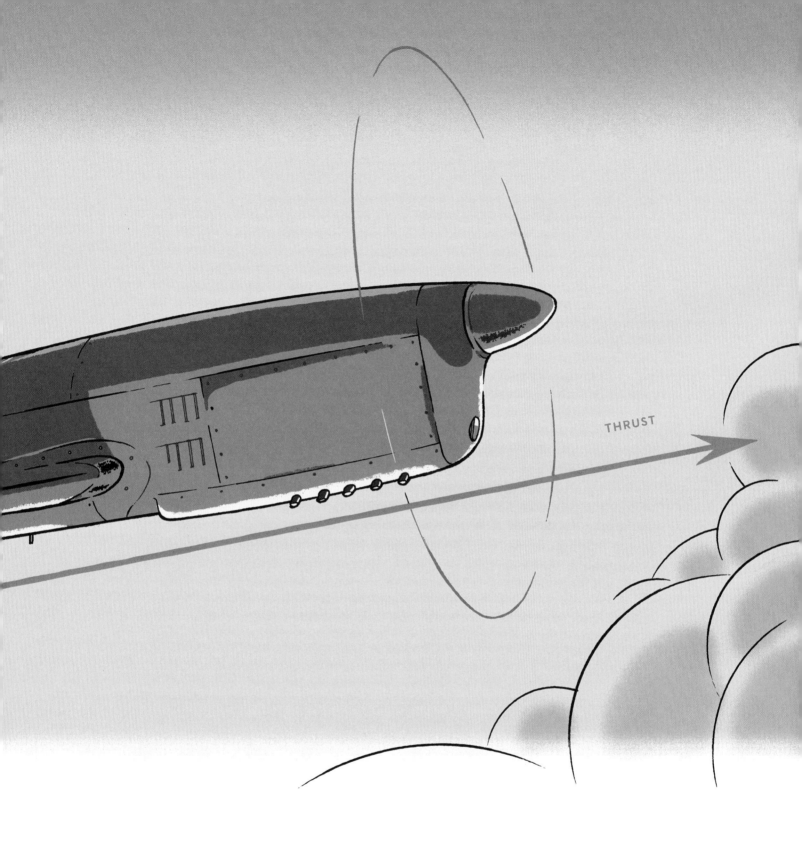

THRUST

pulling the aircraft forward through the air. As the air flows over the wings, the upward force called lift is generated. Lift keeps the airplane in the air.

The balance between these helpful and unhelpful forces determines how the plane will move. When the aircraft flies straight ahead, the forces remain evenly balanced, or in equilibrium. But when the airplane ascends or descends,

the balance changes. Descending requires less lift, and the aircraft reduces its height under the influence of gravity. In contrast, ascending requires extra lift which can be managed by increasing thrust. Some types of aircraft can even climb vertically. A rotor (or rotating wings) pulls the aircraft straight upwards!

IN THE SPOTLIGHT: RENAUD CAUDRON C.460 / 1934

The Caudron C.460 is a French racing aircraft built in 1934 for the Coupe Deutsch de la Meurthe, an international flying competition. The wooden aircraft won the race and broke speed records thanks to the flying skills of Europe's first women pilots. In 1934, Hélène Boucher reached a speed of 455 kilometers an hour (284 mph)! In 1936, the Caudron flew to the United States, where it took part in the National Air Races, a popular competition in the early days of aviation. The aircraft won two trophies there, along with various prizes at other events.

The National Air Races were not just popular spectator events. They were also intended to promote the development of aviation technology. The Caudron excited many people, including Hergé, the cartoonist who created the

famous comic book series *The Adventures of Tintin*. He featured the airplane in a volume from another of his cartoon series called *Jo, Zette, and Jocko*. In this volume, "Mr. Pump's Legacy," engineer Jacques Legrand has to design an aircraft that can fly from Paris to New York at a speed of 1,000 kilometers per hour (more than 600 mph). Hergé's fictional aircraft, the Stratocruiser H.22, is clearly based on the Caudron C.460. Even though the real Caudron couldn't reach 1,000 kilometers per hour, its astonishing speed and streamlined body must have inspired Hergé.

In 2009, an impressive replica of the Caudron C.460 was built by Tom Wathen, Mark Lightsey, Aerocraftsman Inc., and students at Wathen Aviation High School in Riverside, California.

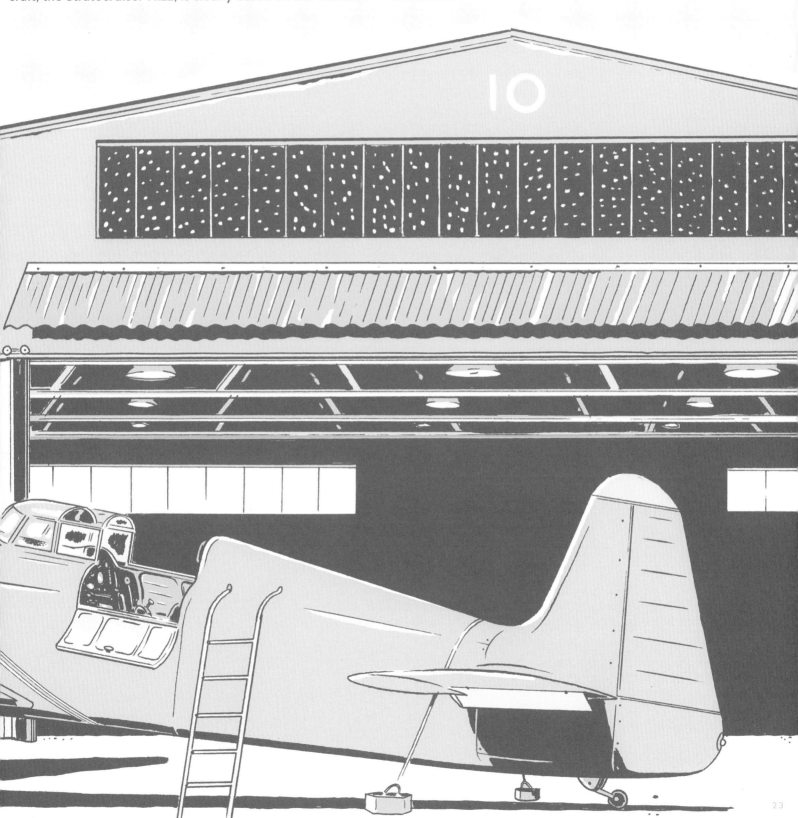

HOW DOES AN AIRPLANE MOVE THROUGH THE AIR?

Airplanes are true acrobats of the skies. To see more clearly all the ways that an airplane moves, we can draw three imaginary lines through the craft. The airplane can turn about each of these three axes. That's how pilots control the direction of flight.

The first imaginary axis passes through the aircraft vertically, from top to bottom. When the airplane rotates about that axis, its nose moves left or right. This is called yawing. The second axis passes horizontally through the aircraft along the wings. When the airplane rotates about this line, its nose moves up or down. This is called pitching. The third and final axis also passes through the aircraft horizontally, but from forward to aft (front to back). When the airplane rotates around that axis, one wing

goes up and the other goes down. This is called rolling. The pilot controls the airplane by combining these three motions. There is a rudder at the tail, which the pilot controls with pedals, causing the airplane to yaw. The airplane pitches when the pilot moves the elevators (horizontal surfaces at the rear of the tail). At the ends of the wings are ailerons, which make it possible for the airplane to roll.

Airplanes are sensitive, and flying them takes great precision. Pilots have to use the controls with great care. The farther they move the flight control surfaces (ailerons, elevators, and rudder), the more extreme the motion of the airplane becomes around the three axes. (Those control actions also affect one another.)

IN THE SPOTLIGHT: LEVASSEUR PL.8 / 1927

Known affectionately as "The White Bird," the Levasseur PL.8 was a unique aircraft. It was flown by Charles Nungesser and François Coli in an attempt to cross the Atlantic Ocean by air for the first time. In a race against the clock, it was supposed to land in the United States twelve days before another pilot, Charles Lindbergh, attempted the same historic feat.

On May 8, 1927, the White Bird took off from Le Bourget Field in France, bound for New York on a route that would have taken it over Ireland, Nova Scotia, and Boston. The landing gear was jettisoned because it was creating too much drag. But this didn't matter much, as the fuselage was designed to act as a boat so it could make a water landing near the Statue of Liberty. The flight was expected to take

42 hours and no longer, as the engine would only keep working without maintenance for 50 hours.
But the aircraft vanished. It was last spotted over Étretat in Northwest France, flying toward England. Witnesses on the island of Saint Pierre, off the coast of Newfoundland, Canada, testified that early in the morning they had heard the noise of the aircraft, followed by a loud bang. The United States Coast Guard is said to have found twisted metal debris from the airplane.

By then, Lindbergh was celebrating his successful transatlantic flight to Paris. Only twenty-five years old, he had built his more modern monoplane himself. Lindbergh became the symbol of a new generation of airplane designers and pilots.

WING SHAPES

An airplane flies thanks to lift, the force that pushes it up into the air. Lift is created by the shape of the wings and by the engine. The engine generates thrust, which sets the airplane in motion so that air flows around the wings. Some of this air flows over the upper surface of the wings. The rest of the air flows under the wings' lower surface.

Because of the shape of the wing, the air moving along the upper surface has farther to go than the air moving along the lower surface. This results in lower pressure on the top of the wing and higher pressure on the bottom, lifting the airplane. Other wing shapes do not have the same effect. They disrupt the flow of air but do not create lift.

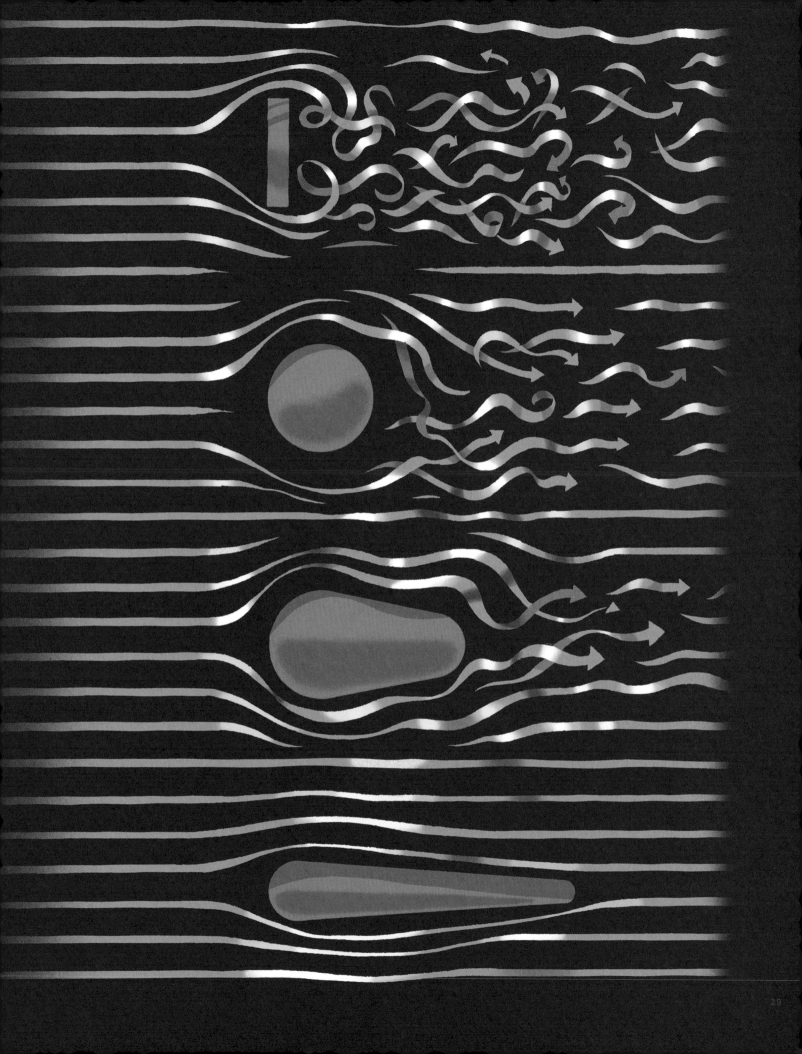

A FLYING WING

We have seen that a wing creates lift and very little drag. So what if you build an airplane that's nothing but a wing? Jack Northrop designed one in the 1930s. The body, engines, fuel, cargo, and pilot were all packed into that one large, flying wing. The hope was that this flying wing would have a great deal of upward lift and encounter very little air resistance. The plan worked, but the design ran into quite a few other problems. The aircraft was unstable and difficult to control. Even experienced test pilots could barely manage to fly it. Because it had no tail, the flight control surfaces all had to be attached to the wing, so the airplane was constantly making uncontrolled movements.

A later version of this aircraft, called the YB-49, had a tragic ending. It crashed in 1948, killing pilot Daniel Forbes and

co-pilot Glen Edwards. Both of these brave pilots have United States Air Force bases named after them.
The flying wing design actually came a little too early in aviation history—at a time when propeller-driven airplanes were beginning to be replaced by a new generation of aircraft with jet engines. Aircraft technology was not yet sufficient to fix the problems of the early flying wings, which were never perfectly reliable. Eventually, the whole project had to be abandoned.

IN THE SPOTLIGHT: NORTHROP YB-35 FLYING WING / 1946

A flying wing was the dream design and life's work of American aeronautics engineer Jack Northrop, but his idea was not unique. In Germany, the Horten brothers were also designing flying wings; and the basic design had actually been conceived in 1910 by British engineer John William Dunne.

Nevertheless, Northrop became the first engineer to make the idea work in practice. He designed several models, including a small one-person glider, a version with four pairs of propellers (the YB-35), and an airplane 52.4 meters (172 feet) wide, driven by eight jet engines (the YB-49). These were intended for use as reconnaissance aircraft by the United States Air Force, but during the initial tests all the orders were cancelled.

The flying wings were seen as too unreliable, and they were completely disassembled before the eyes of Northrop and his employees. Jack Northrop looked on in dismay as his life's work was destroyed. But his genius would eventually lead to new advances in aircraft technology.

In April 1980, the elderly Northrop was taken to an office in the company he had established years earlier and shown a model of the B-2 Spirit bomber, an aircraft based entirely on his original design. Deeply moved, Northrop said, "Now I know why God has kept me alive for the past twenty-five years."

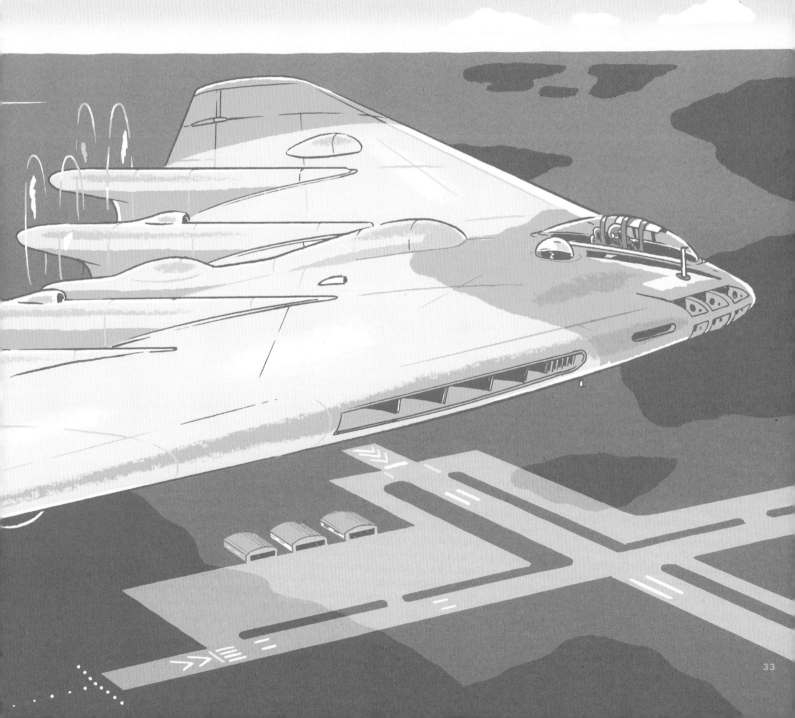

AN INVISIBLE FLYING WING

The B-2, known in full as the Northrop Grumman B-2, saw the light of day in 1970. Engineers had taken a fresh look at the findings from flying wing test flights in the 1940s and discovered that the design could be used for a new type of bomber. The new aircraft even had the same wingspan as the original design. The original prototype had been difficult to control, but later technology solved that problem and made this type of aircraft manageable for pilots.

The new technology was named fly-by-wire. With it, the pilot could use a computer (or Flight Control System) to manipulate the aircraft's control surfaces so that the plane would do what the pilot wished. The system gave pilots more control over these large, complex flying machines.

Airplanes like the B-2 are also designed to be invisible to

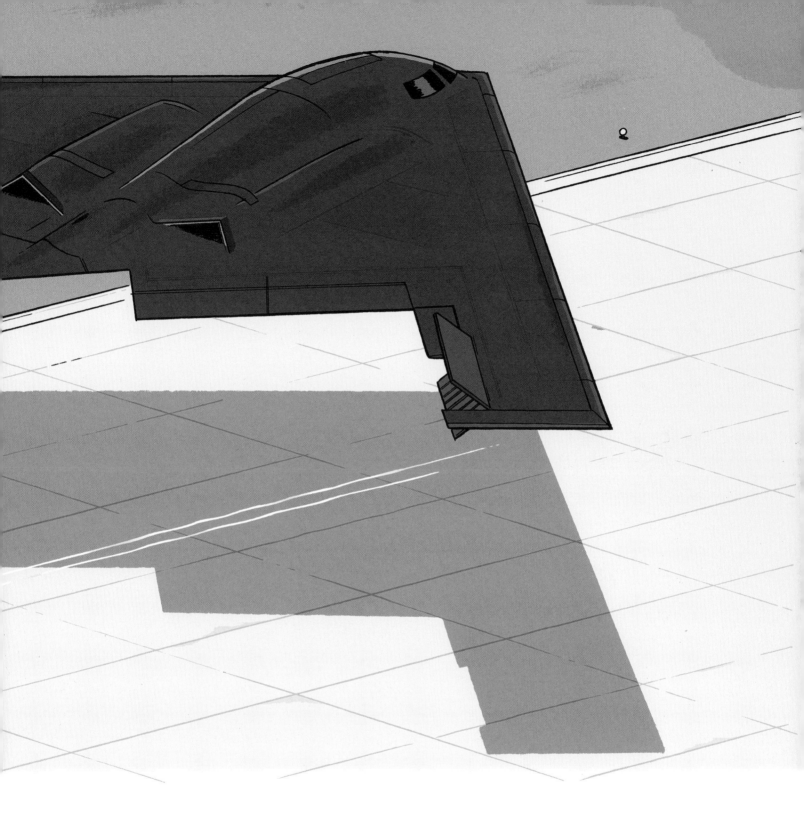

radar. Known as stealth aircraft, they have all the same parts as an ordinary plane, but these parts are moved from the outside to the inside. Thanks to the unusual shape of the B-2, as well as its concealed exhaust ducts and its specially-formulated paint, the aircraft can reflect radar energy in a different way. This makes the airplane completely invisible on radar screens and to air traffic controllers.

The B-2 has room for two people. It can reach an altitude of 15,000 meters (50,000 feet) and fly distances of more than 10,000 kilometers (more than 6,000 miles). It's not fast, but it doesn't have to be. It's an espionage aircraft and always has its trump card: invisibility. Its air intakes and other protruding parts are shaped like swept (tilted) diamonds, which make them less detectable by radar.

The B-2 can fly over countries unnoticed and observe what is happening on the ground. When they fly very high, however, they can leave white trails of condensation known as contrails. The water vapor in their exhaust fumes freezes, leaving behind a long, line-shaped cloud. To avoid this problem, the B-2 has a system that warns the pilots in the cockpit when they are at risk of leaving a contrail. The pilots can then fly

lower and prevent the aircraft from being detected. These high-tech airplanes are expensive, and only twenty have been built. They are literally worth their weight in gold, so you're not likely to see a B-2 flying in your neighborhood. You can, however, admire the one on display in the National Museum of the United States Air Force in Dayton, Ohio. There were espionage aircraft even before the development of the B-2, but they were detectable by radar. All the same, they were remarkable airplanes. For example, the Lockheed U-2 could fly at an altitude of 21,000 meters (69,000 feet), and the Lockheed SR-71 Blackbird could reach a velocity of 3,500 kilometers per hour (2,200 mph)—literally faster than a speeding bullet!

FLYING WITHOUT WINGS

As we've already seen, some planes are designed in the form of one large wing. But can you also fly without wings? Researchers began looking into that possibility in the 1960s for the purpose of space travel. To fly into outer space, a craft has to maintain a high speed, but that creates enormous friction. Friction generates heat, a phenomenon you can feel if you rub your hands together fast. To avoid the dangers of excess heat, a spacecraft has to have a streamlined body with little or no wings. This type of design is sometimes called a lifting body.

The wings of traditional airplanes generate the most lift when travelling at subsonic speeds. But lifting bodies create more lift at higher speeds. Their shape ensures their stability. The pressure on the lower surface of the aircraft is greater

than that on the upper surface. This is the source of the lift. And that is how the first spacecraft came into being. Since no one really knew how they would behave in flight, the first ones built were small-scale models, tested in a wind tunnel. Like other aircraft with unconventional shapes, lifting bodies proved difficult to control. They handled well at high speeds, but at lower speeds they were unmanageable. Because of this problem, spacecraft were ultimately designed with short, triangular delta wings.

The Northrop HL-10's strange shape earned it the name of the Flying Bathtub. It was one of five experimental lifting bodies tested by the American space agency NASA. The aircraft were tested at Edwards Air Force Base in California in a spectacular way. The earliest prototypes had no engines of their own but were towed by a car over the large, flat expanse of a dried-up lake. Later, they were mounted below the right wing of a much larger aircraft. When that craft reached an altitude of 15 kilometers (50,000 feet), it would release the Northrop HL-10. The pilot of the HL-10 would then start the engine, and the vehicle would rise to an altitude of 24 kilometers (80,000 feet), where it would run out of fuel and its engine would shut down. Next, the pilot would fly downwards at a steep angle, so that the craft would

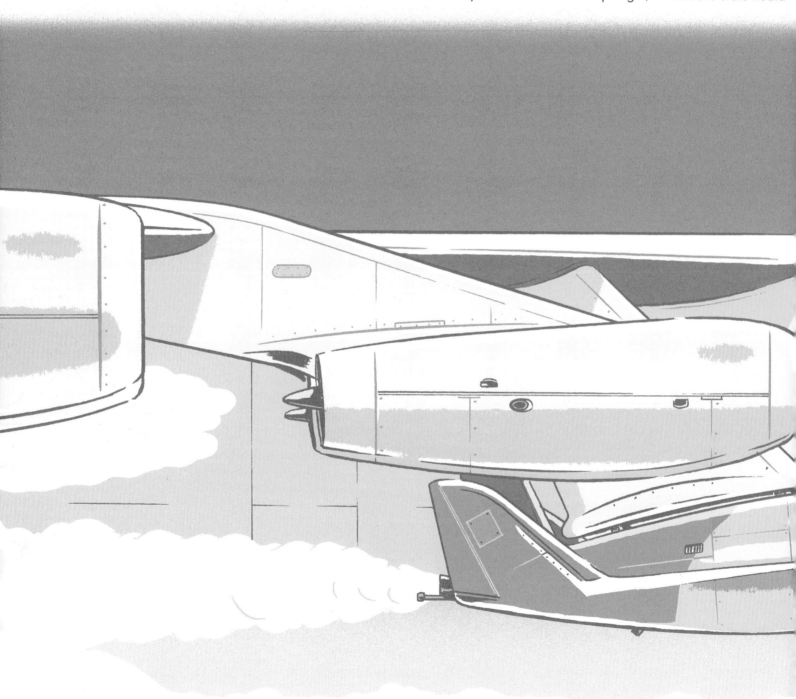

keep moving fast enough to remain controllable until just before it landed.

These flights never lasted long; there was enough fuel on board to ascend for about one hundred seconds. The longest of the thirty-seven HL–10 test flights took only seven minutes. The vehicle landed in the dried-up lake at Edwards Air Force Base at a speed of 300 kilometers per hour (190 mph).

These experimental, glider-like vehicles led to the development of the space shuttle, which also re-entered the atmosphere much like a glider after its missions in outer space!

THE GROUND EFFECT

A wing close to the ground behaves differently than one in full flight. When an airplane flies lower than 5 meters (16 feet) above the ground, it creates the ground effect, or cushion effect. Because the air below the wing can no longer escape, it forms a kind of cushion over which the aircraft glides. Pilots can use the cushion effect to bring the airplane to a soft landing.

Some vehicles, like the Ekranoplan, take advantage of this phenomenon in a clever way. Their wings are designed so that they can fly no higher than the range of the ground effect. This effect, however, is not convenient for every aircraft. Gliders have long wings designed so they can glide as far as possible without descending. That feature sometimes makes it hard for them to land; they just keep on gliding. To

take care of that problem, they have devices called spoilers that disrupt the flow of air over the wing, reducing lift and making it possible for the aircraft to land.

The animal kingdom also takes advantage of the ground effect. Daubenton's bats use much less energy when they fly close to the surface of the water, which keeps their heart rate low, especially when the water surface is calm and ripple-free. Sea birds such as albatrosses and pelicans also benefit from the ground effect.

IN THE SPOTLIGHT: EKRANOPLAN A-90 ORLYONOK / 1960

The Ekranoplan, also known as the Caspian Sea Monster, was a watercraft intended to exploit the ground effect to its fullest. It was designed in 1960 by the Russian engineer Rostislav Alekseyev, who had also designed hovercrafts, another type of vehicle that uses cushions of air. Looking like a cross between a hovercraft and an airplane, the Ekranoplan glided over the water at a height of 5 meters (16 feet) above ground level. The engines were in front, in the nose, and they blew air under the wings. On its tail was the most powerful turboprop engine ever built, which gave the aircraft its speed. The Ekranoplan did not have an attractive appearance, as its "monstrous" nickname suggests. But its efficient design enabled it to transport huge quantities of cargo over water quickly. As long as the vehicle remained just

above the surface of the water, the ground effect allowed it to operate without using much energy.

The Ekranoplan glided over the Caspian Sea at a speed of 400 kilometers per hour (249 mph). And because it flew so low, it remained undetectable by radar. Flying low, however, also had disadvantages. Pilots would have to keep a very careful watch on the horizon to avoid collisions with ships.

Because of their low flying height, ground effect vehicles are registered as ships rather than as airplanes. After the breakup of the Soviet Union, there was less interest in the Caspian Sea Monsters and less money available for building them. Ekranoplans are no longer used.

HOW DO AILERONS WORK?

When pilots want to make a turn, they use their ailerons—moving parts on the trailing edge of the outer wings. The pilot shifts the control stick or wheel to the left or right to adjust the ailerons' position.

A plane's two ailerons go in opposite directions; when one moves upwards, the other moves downwards. When the pilot makes a right turn, the left aileron goes down. That movement changes the shape of the left wing slightly, giving it more lift, so that the left side of the aircraft rises. At the same time, the right aileron goes up, lowering the craft's right wing. The imbalance in the wings increases, and the airplane moves to the right.

But making a turn is not as simple as it sounds. When the left wing rises, it encounters more air resistance. That causes

the nose to pull against the turn—in this case, to the left. This unwanted effect is called adverse yaw. A pilot can overcome adverse yaw by operating the rudder with pedals. The rudder forces the nose of the aircraft to point in the right direction, permitting a graceful, coordinated turn.

As you can see, flying is a little bit like driving: you need to use your hands and feet at the same time.

IN THE SPOTLIGHT: PIPER WARRIOR P-28 A / 1960

Piper, like Cessna, Grumman, and Beechcraft, is a manufacturer of smaller aircraft for many aviation academies and private owners. Since it was founded in 1927, Piper has built thousands of airplanes, most of which are still flying. In 1937, the company developed the Piper Cub, an aircraft designed to encourage everyone to fly.

The Piper Warrior is the aircraft on which many pilots learn to fly. It's the ideal trainer craft, forgiving of mistakes. Piper Warriors are low-wing airplanes, with tapered wings designed to have a slight twist that makes them easier to control (a phenomenon called washout). The Lycoming engine is rated at 160 horsepower and gives the airplane a maximum speed of 217 kilometers per hour (135 mph). On a full tank, the Warrior can travel 950 kilometers

(590 miles) in five hours with a forty-five minute reserve. It can climb to an altitude of 3.3 kilometers (more than 10,000 feet) and requires a distance of about 500 meters (1,640 feet) to ascend 15 meters (50 feet).

There are many Piper Warriors in the air, but no two are alike. Each pilot can equip the airplane with extra instruments, radio apparatus, and navigation devices. But these additions can increase the plane's weight, and having more electrical instruments can interfere with the compass readings. Altered Piper Warriors often have to be re-inspected. Their weight, center of gravity, and balance are then recalculated, and their compass is recalibrated.

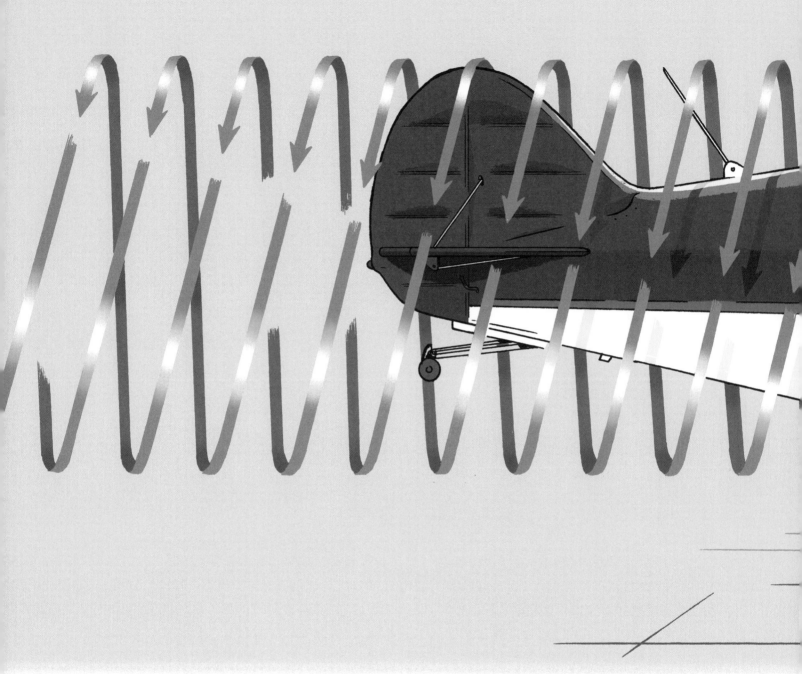

THE AIRPLANE PROPELLER

The propeller of an airplane is essentially a kind of wing. It has two or more blades around a rotating hub. If you sawed through one of the blades, you would see that the cross-section looks a lot like the cross-section of a wing. When these "mini-wings" spin, they create a current of air moving backwards, which curls around the plane like a corkscrew. In other words, the propeller not only pushes the air backwards but also makes it whirl around in a spiral. That action converts the power of the engine into thrust, one of the four main forces described on page 20.

The advantage of the corkscrew-shaped current of air is that it passes quickly over the elevator and rudder, keeping these control surfaces efficient and easy for the pilot to maneuver, even at slower speeds. The ailerons are at the outer ends of

the wings, so they do not benefit from this corkscrew-shaped propeller blast.

In 1944 Curtis Pitts designed the Pitts Special, a series of biplanes intended for aerobatics, or fancy maneuvers in the air. The earliest Specials were decorated with a picture of a skunk. In 1950, this model aroused the interest of the general public when stunt pilot Betty Skelton became America's female aerobatic champion for the third year in a row. She called her Pitts "Little Stinker."

The biplane is the gold standard for aerobatics. Biplanes have two sets of short wings. That makes them especially easy to maneuver. Biplanes are also exceptionally endurable. They have to be, because aerial stunts challenge them in unusual ways. Stunt planes, for example, have to deal with powerful gravitational forces called g-forces. The Pitts can handle forces from +6 g to -5 g. At +6 g, pilots are pressed

into the seat as if their body weighed six times as much as they do on land. At -5 g, the force pushes pilots out of their seats with five times the force of their body weight.

Stunt flying is a discipline in itself. Judges decide on a sequence of maneuvers to be performed. The pilot who flies the sequence best wins the trophy. Some stunt pilots have upside-down lettering on their fuselage, as they spend more time flying upside down than right side up!

The Pitts Special has a steel tube frame, but the rest is made of wood and solid fabric. If you tap on the wings, the taut fabric sounds almost like a drum. Pitts sold his company in 1977, and by 1981 the plane was being built at a company owned by Frank Christensen. That history explains the aircraft's current double name, "Christen Pitts."

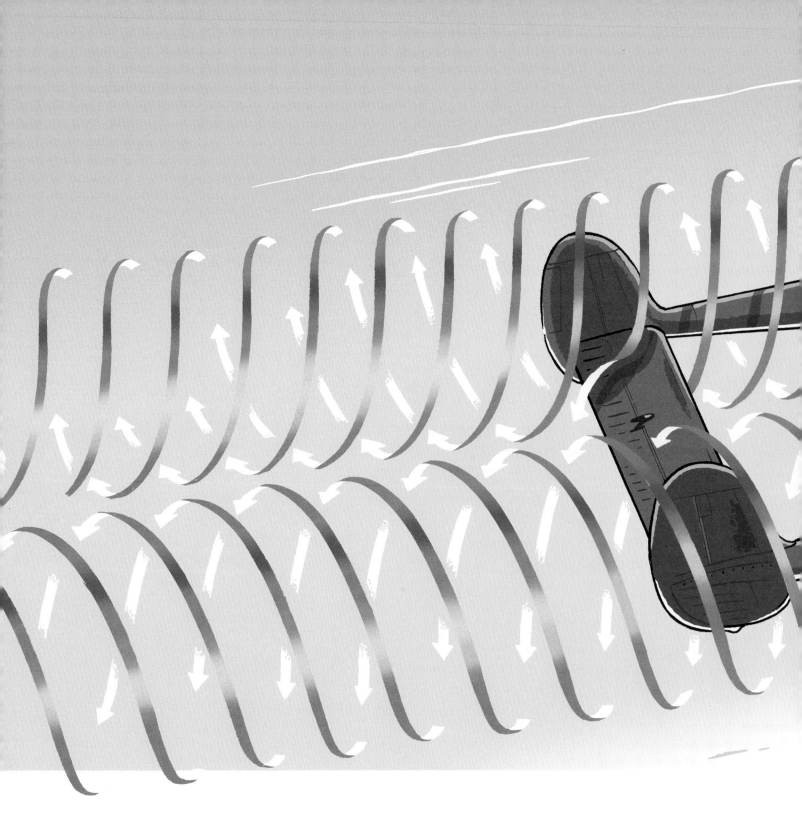

THE DOUBLE PROPELLER

You don't have to limit yourself to a single propeller. The year 1941 saw the introduction of the first airplane with two propellers. The U.S. Air Force wanted a fighter aircraft that could attain a velocity of 580 km/h (360 mph) at a height of 6,000 meters (20,000 feet). The result was the Lockheed P-38 Lightning.

As its name suggests, the Lightning was one of the fastest

airplanes of its day. In 1939, a prototype set a speed record by flying from California to New York in seven hours and two minutes. Its strong twin engines each had a horsepower of more than 1,000. The engines were water-cooled and so large and powerful that they were housed in two separate bodies, called booms, connected by a central cockpit in front and at the tail. That arrangement gave the P-38 Lightning

a distinctive outline against the sky. The pilot sat on top of the plane, so to speak, between the two booms, and had an excellent view of the surroundings.

When the two engines, and therefore the two propellers, turned in the same direction, the tail of the aircraft received a tremendous push. This feature made the P–38 difficult to maneuver. The attempted solution was to make the engines

turn in opposite directions. However, counter-rotating engines require extra maintenance and more spare parts, and keeping the P–38 in perfect condition was difficult and expensive. For financial reasons, the air forces that used this craft opted for engines that rotated in the same direction.

IN THE SPOTLIGHT: LOCKHEED P-38 LIGHTNING / 1941

The P-38 Lightning was one of the most successful aircraft in the Second World War, flown by many famous pilots. After crossing the Atlantic, Charles Lindbergh became an expert in energy-efficient flying. He advised pilots on how to use the Lightning's powerful engines as sparingly as possible. French author Antoine de Saint-Exupéry, best known for the poetic tale *The Little Prince*, also flew a P–38. But his career as a pilot in the French Air Force ended in disaster. On July 31, 1944, he left Corsica to conduct an unarmed photographic reconnaissance mission over southern France. Antoine de Saint-Exupéry disappeared along with his airplane. Not until 2000 was part of the aircraft found, along with the pilot's identity bracelet, in the sea off the coast of Marseille. Four years later, it was confirmed that both the wreckage and

bracelet had come from Saint-Exupéry's P–38.
Was it engine trouble, oxygen deprivation, or a desperate
act? The pilot's fate remains unclear.

HOW DO FLAPS WORK?

We have seen that the ailerons, depending on their position, can adjust the wings separately and send the airplane in a certain direction. But there are other moving parts attached to the wings: devices called flaps. If you have ever sat close to the wing on an airliner, you may have seen them sliding in and out. They can make the wing surface larger or smaller. That ability gives airplanes flying at low speeds sufficient lift

and helps them remain stable in the air.

Flaps are especially important for firefighting aircraft, sometimes called airtankers or water bombers. These planes have to scoop up large amounts of water and then ascend rapidly despite the extra weight. To perform such a difficult feat, firefighting planes such as the Canadair are equipped with huge flaps on large wings. The flaps are so large that the

craft needs a larger tail assembly to remain in balance. The flaps also help the plane as it flies over the fire, where the air is very turbulent and unstable. The aircraft can continue flying slowly without losing lift or stability, giving the pilot enough time to drop the water and put out the flames. Some airplanes have other parts on their wings that enable them to fly more effectively. Retractable devices called slats along the edge of the wing are used together with the flaps to maintain lift at slower speeds.

IN THE SPOTLIGHT: CANADAIR CL-415 / 1967

The Canadair CL-415, the new version of the original Canadair CL-215, is the ultimate aircraft for putting out forest fires. The tank on this firefighting machine holds 6,000 liters (more than 1,500 gallons) of water and can be filled in twelve seconds. Canadair CL-415s scoop up the water from natural sources, such as rivers or lakes, near the fire. These sources can be as little as 2 meters (6 feet) deep, but they must be at least 2 kilometers (1.2 miles) long. The aircraft often fill their tanks very close to ships or beachgoers.

According to legend, swimmers are sometimes scooped up accidentally and later found in the area where the fire was put out. But that story isn't possible in real life! The openings connected to the tanks are too small. If they were large enough for swimmers to pass through, the aircraft would get

stuck on the surface of the water and pitch down when it tried to take off.

Flying a Canadair over a forest fire is dangerous. Only an elite group of very experienced pilots, mostly ex-military individuals, is allowed to fly the 125 planes that have been built. You can see Canadairs in real life at Winnipeg-James Armstrong Richardson Airport in Winnipeg, Canada. They are also used in France, Greece, Spain, and Turkey.

In April 2019, when a fire broke out at Notre-Dame cathedral in Paris, some people wondered why the firefighters didn't use a Canadair. These planes, however, are not designed for that type of fire. They release water with such force that it would have done structural damage to the church.

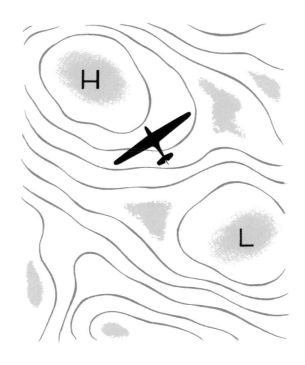

ATMOSPHERE AND WEATHER

AN AIRPLANE'S HABITAT

exosphere
500–1,000 km (311–621 miles)

International Space Station
330–410 km (186–255 miles)

thermosphere
85–500 km (53–311 miles)

Northern Lights
Aurora Borealis
80–1,000 km (50–621 miles)

mesosphere
50–80 km (31–50 miles)

stratosphere 12–50 km (7.5–31 miles)

tropopause 12 km (7.5 miles)

troposphere 0–12 km (0–7.5 miles)

THE ATMOSPHERE

From the Earth, outer space seems far away; but from space, the layer of air around the Earth looks very thin. It protects us from harmful cosmic rays and from the sun.

The lowest layer, up to about 12 kilometers (7.5 miles) from the Earth's surface, is the troposphere. It contains the clouds, the weather systems, and—up towards the top—the airliners. Here, temperatures drop as you climb higher.

But in the boundary region on top of the troposphere, the temperature barely drops. This region is called the tropopause.

Above the tropopause, temperatures actually increase with altitude. This layer, called the stratosphere, extends from about 12 to 50 kilometers (7.5 to 31 miles) high. At the top, the temperature is about equal to that on the ground.

meteors
60 km (37 miles)

Above the stratosphere is the mesosphere. It begins at a height of 50 kilometers (31 miles), where temperatures start to drop again. At the highest point in the mesosphere, the temperature is -100 °C (-148 °F)! This is also where the Northern Lights form. Charged particles from the sun light up when they collide with particles of oxygen in our atmosphere, producing the Northern Lights' pretty colors.

Above the mesosphere is the thermosphere, where exposure to the sun's radiation produces dramatically higher temperatures—from 1,000 °C (1,800 °F) at night to 1,700 °C (3,100 °F) by day. Here, the International Space Station orbits Earth. The exosphere begins at a height of 500 kilometers (310 miles). Particles here end up lost in the vacuum of outer space.

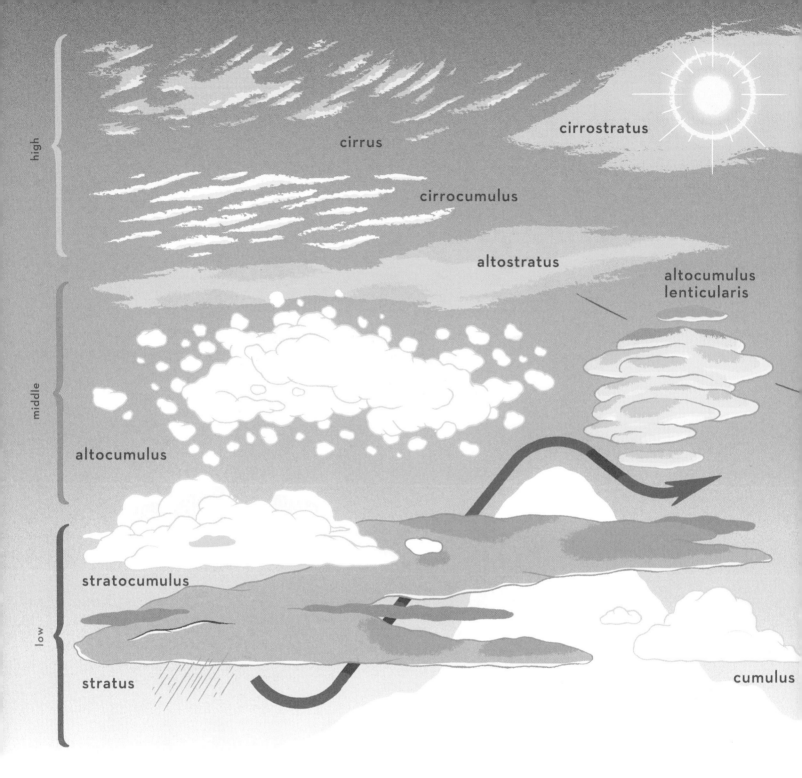

middle

low

cirrus

cirrostratus

cirrocumulus

altostratus

altocumulus
lenticularis

altocumulus

stratocumulus

stratus

cumulus

TYPES OF CLOUDS

If we want to fly safely, it's important to keep a close eye on the weather forecast. Most airplanes fly in the troposphere, the layer of air closest to the Earth's surface. The air in this layer moves, and you can find many clouds there that reveal information about the weather. There are three types of clouds: high, middle, and low. Stratus clouds are typical low-level clouds seen on overcast days with uniform gray skies.

Low cumulus clouds are a sign of good weather. They look like little white balls of cotton in the blue summer sky. At a somewhat higher altitude, stratocumulus clouds can cover a wide area.

Still higher in the atmosphere, we find altostratus, cirro-cumulus, cirrus, and cirrostratus clouds. The ice crystals in this last variety sometimes create a halo around the sun.

cumulonimbus incus

cumulonimbus

Cumulonimbus clouds are an especially notorious variety. Inside them are strong upward air currents that can generate static electricity, which we observe in the form of thunder and lightning. In short, cumulonimbuses are real storm clouds, and airplanes tend to keep their distance from them. Altocumulus lenticularis clouds are an attractive variety found in mountainous regions. They resemble a stack of plates—a feature that has given them their French name: pile d'assiettes. Many people who see them cannot help but think of flying saucers. They are formed from moisture in the flowing air over mountains.

8,000 ft (2,438 m)

7,000 ft (2,134 m)

6,000 ft (1,829 m)

5,000 ft (1524 m)

4,000 ft (1,219 m)

3,000 ft (914 m)

2,000 ft (610 m)

1,000 ft (305 m)

WHAT DOES AIR DO TO AN AIRPLANE?

We cannot see the air around us, yet it is filled with particles. The closer you come to sea level, the larger the number of particles of air suspended above you, and the greater the pressure all those particles exert on you. An airplane that takes off at sea level is flying through the "thickest" air. As it ascends, the air grows thinner and the number of particles pressing down on it decreases. When an airplane flies at a high altitude, where the air is thin, it encounters less air resistance. Using the same amount of energy, it can fly faster at high altitude than it can close to the ground.

At high altitudes, however, there is also less lift, because fewer particles of air flow over the wings. That is why an airplane has a ceiling, a maximum height up to which the wings can carry it. Once it reaches that point, the aircraft cannot

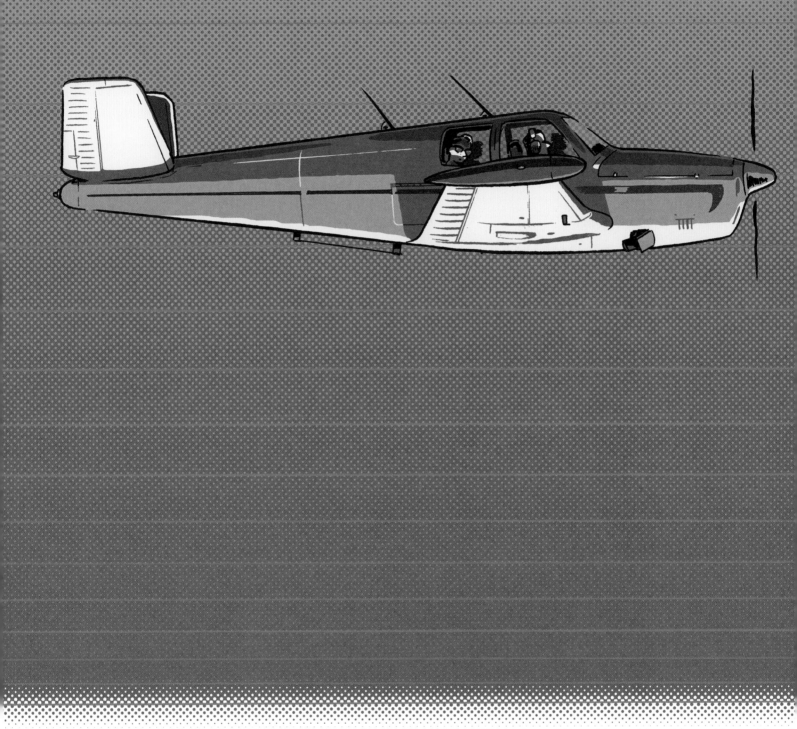

fly any higher. Moreover, planes cannot ascend as quickly at high altitudes as they can at sea level. An airplane taking off from a coastal airport, therefore, can ascend faster and needs less distance than one taking off from an airport in the mountains. Two crucial aspects of taking off are runway length and flying over any obstacles located just past the end of the runway. And there are other factors that influence

aircraft performance. Warm air expands and is thinner than cold air. Thus, an airplane that can take off without any trouble on a cold morning may be more sluggish when getting off the ground on a hot afternoon, even from the same airport. It's important, therefore, for the pilot to be aware of the air pressure. Fortunately, pilots have tables for calculating the exact runway length needed for a safe take-off.

IN THE SPOTLIGHT: BEECHCRAFT BONANZA / 1947

On February 2, 1959, rock stars Buddy Holly, Ritchie Valens, and the Big Bopper (J.P. Richardson) performed at the Surf Ballroom in the U.S. city of Clear Lake, Iowa. Afterwards, the three musicians didn't like the idea of a long, cold bus trip to their next performance, so they decided to rent an airplane. At 1 a.m. on February 3rd, their Beechcraft Bonanza, piloted by Roger Peterson, left Mason City Municipal Airport in Iowa for Hector Airport in North Dakota. But the plane never reached its destination. It was found the next day about 8 kilometers (5 miles) from the take-off runway. Shortly after departure, it had flown into a snowstorm.

The pilot was unable to see through the window, and he had been forced to rely completely on his instruments. But Peterson had little experience with 'blind flying.' Soon after

take-off, he became disoriented and the airplane crashed. The crash that killed the three rock stars went down in history as The Day the Music Died. The Beechcraft Bonanza has been a popular aircraft among private pilots and charter companies; some 17,000 have been built. But the three musicians were not the only ones to crash in a Bonanza. Apple co-founder Steve Wozniak survived a crash in his Bonanza on February 7, 1981. The country singer Jim Reeves died in an accident in 1964 and American rock guitarist Randy Rhoads was killed in 1982, each in a Beechcraft Bonanza.

TURBULENCE AND THERMALS

On warm days, the air becomes turbulent and thermals form. The sun warms the Earth's surface, which in turn warms the air above it. Turbulence and thermals take place more often above warm areas, such as industrial sites. They occur much less often over cooler areas, such as forests and ponds. Air rises as it grows warmer. This creates a current of rising air, which we call a thermal. The larger the difference in temperature between the rising air and the surrounding atmosphere, the stronger the current. At great heights, the air is colder. Then the water vapor in the rising current condenses, forming clouds. Besides these moist thermals, there are also dry thermals. If the rising air is too dry, then no clouds will form.

When an airplane flies through an unstable air layer, it usually

experiences turbulence and is shaken severely. But a glider takes advantage of this phenomenon; the pilot seeks out thermals by circling over warm areas. Thanks to the aircraft's long wings, it can soar on the rising current of air, flying even higher and farther without an engine. The pilot uses the thermal to gain altitude and then glides off to another area with many thermals.

"Thermalling" inside a warm bubble of air can be hard work, because the wind can blow the bubble away. Fortunately, pilots receive help from birds, which are master gliders and know just how to soar on the rising currents of air. By watching birds, glider pilots can locate bubbles of warm air that they can use to stay aloft.

IN THE SPOTLIGHT: DFS HABICHT / 1936

The DFS Habicht (German for "Hawk") was a stunt glider designed by Hans Jacobs. It was intended to impress visitors to the Berlin Olympic Games in 1936. One of these wooden gliders (only four were built in the 1930s) performed acrobatic feats over the Olympic stadium. Pilots like Hanna Retch praised the Habicht for its maneuverability and handling qualities.

The airplane had a wingspan of 13.6 meters (44 feet 7 inches), short for a glider, so it was sturdy and had a good, fast roll rate. The craft could handle g-forces from +12 g to -9 g. Those are extremely powerful forces, if you consider that any force above or below +1 g has a noticeable effect.
A modified version of the airplane had even shorter wings and was dubbed the Stummel-Habicht ("Stumpy Hawk").

It was used to teach young German pilots to fly the Messer-schmitt ME 163 Komet, a rocket-powered fighter craft. This is because the Komet landed at high speed, just like the Stummel-Habicht.

Only one Habicht survived the Second World War. It was put on display in the Paris aviation museum. But copies were built by Josef Kurz and other members of the Oldtimer Segelflugclub Wasserkuppe, a German association dedicated to keeping the history of glider aircraft alive. This accomplishment was especially remarkable because the original design documents had been lost. Later on, another Habicht was made by Dieter Kemler and the Zahn family. So today there are three Habicht airplanes in existence!

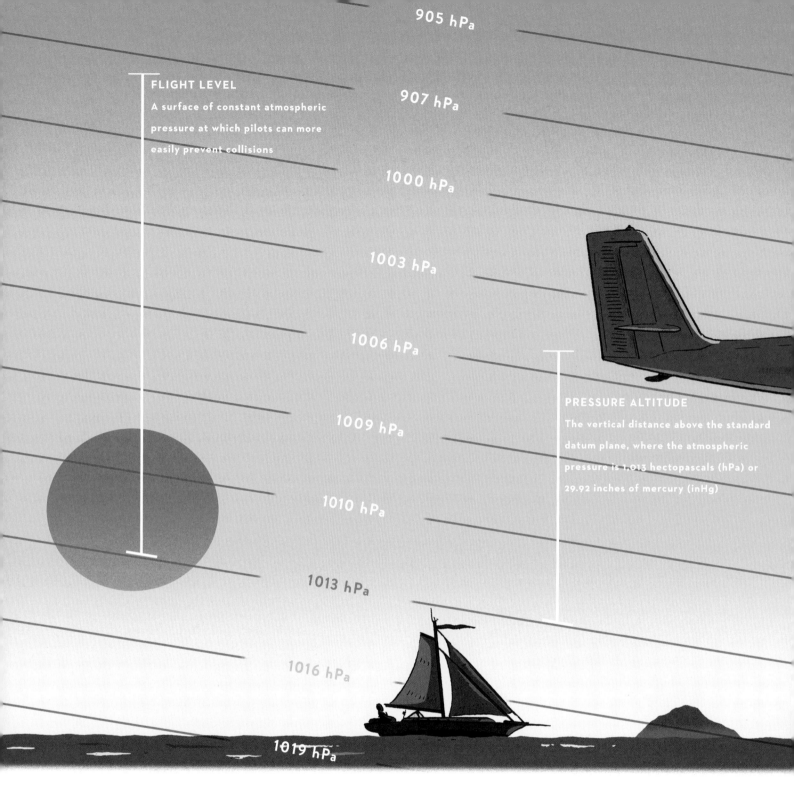

905 hPa

FLIGHT LEVEL
A surface of constant atmospheric
pressure at which pilots can more
easily prevent collisions

907 hPa

1000 hPa

1003 hPa

1006 hPa

1009 hPa

PRESSURE ALTITUDE
The vertical distance above the standard
datum plane, where the atmospheric
pressure is 1,013 hectopascals (hPa) or
29.92 inches of mercury (inHg)

1010 hPa

1013 hPa

1016 hPa

1019 hPa

THE ALTIMETER

With altimeters, pilots determine their planes' exact altitude
by measuring the pressure of their surrounding atmosphere.
In general, as you fly higher the surrounding air pressure
descends. But air pressure is not the same everywhere in
the world, so there was a need for a standard pressure that
could apply to all altimeters. The model adopted worldwide
is called the International Standard Atmosphere (ISA). The

standard pressure value is 1,013 hPa (1.013 bar) at sea level at
a temperature of 15 °C (59 °F).

Just before departure, a pilot is informed of the local air
pressure and uses it to calibrate the altimeter. Once in
flight, the pilot then knows the height of the aircraft relative
to the take-off runway. But local air pressure at the destination often differs from that at the point of departure, so

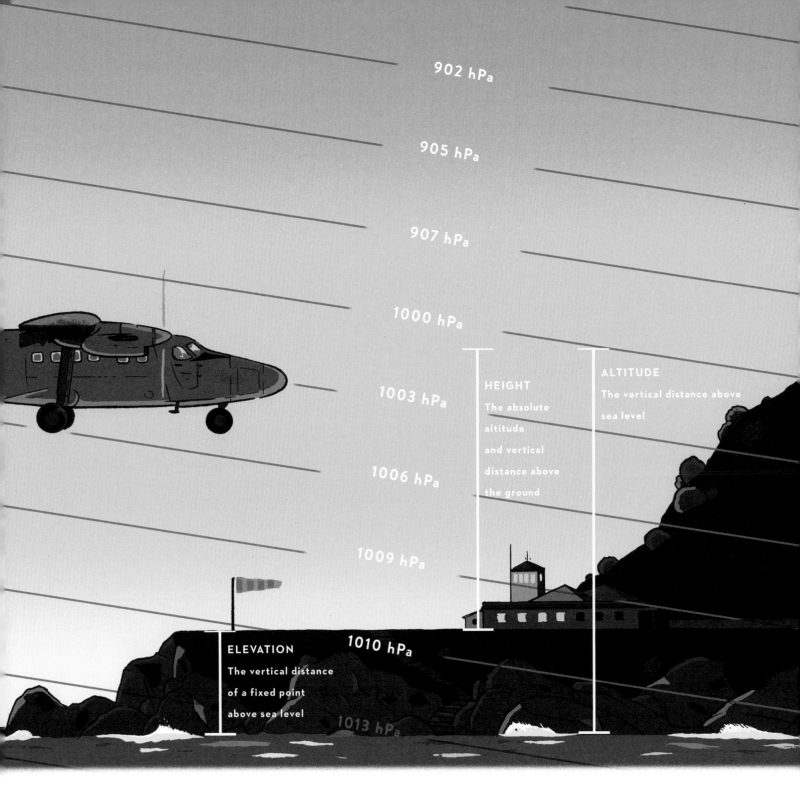

902 hPa

905 hPa

907 hPa

1000 hPa

1003 hPa

HEIGHT
The absolute
altitude
and vertical
distance above
the ground

ALTITUDE
The vertical distance above
sea level

1006 hPa

1009 hPa

ELEVATION
The vertical distance
of a fixed point
above sea level

1010 hPa

1013 hPa

it's important for the pilot to make the adjustment before landing. If, for example, the destination is at a higher elevation than the point of departure, the pilot adjusts the altimeter so the plane doesn't fly too low and risk crashing. On long, high-altitude flights, all altimeters are set to the ISA value, rather than local atmospheric pressure. High-flying pilots measure altitude in "flight levels," or the aircraft's

altitude at standard air pressure at sea level. Flight level 100 (FL100) stands for an altitude of 10,000 feet (3,048 meters). Other nearby airplanes then have to stay at a maximum altitude of FL95 or a minimum altitude of FL105. By using this system, pilots can keep track of their vertical distance from each other, maintaining a difference of at least 500 feet (about 150 meters).

IN THE SPOTLIGHT: DE HAVILLAND CANADA DHC-6 TWIN OTTER / 1965

Suppose you want to fly to the Caribbean island of Saba. Only 13 square kilometers (5 square miles) in area, it has one of the world's two shortest runways. The other one is at Matekane Airport in the Southern African nation of Lesotho. Saba's runway strip is 400 meters (1,312 feet) long. Planes fly to this airport from the neighboring island of Sint Maarten. As an aircraft lands in Saba, waves and rocks come uncomfortably close; the plane almost seems to come to a stop, hovering at the start of the landing strip. Before you know it, the aircraft has landed on one of the world's scariest runways, and everyone can breathe again.

What makes this dramatic landing possible is the Twin Otter. This small, twin-engine airplane was designed to transport eighteen passengers and two pilots to places that

are difficult to reach. Known as a short take-off and landing (STOL) aircraft, the Twin Otter can serve as an ambulance, a seaplane, a skiplane, or a bush airplane. It flies not only between the Caribbean islands, but also in Alaska, Antarctica, and between different Pacific islands. To use the Saba airport, pilots need specialized training and a prestigious license.

The Twin Otter is also an ideal rescue plane that can fly in inhospitable areas. It served as a rescue plane for the third time in 2016, when two workers at a South Pole research station needed urgent medical treatment. Flying to the South Pole would be impossible for any other airplane from March to October, when utter darkness reigns and the temperature can drop as low as -80 °C (-112 °F).

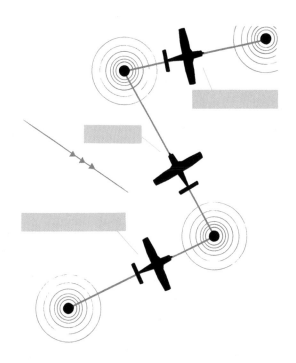

COMMUNICATION AND NAVIGATION

MANAGING AIRSPACE

COMMUNICATION BY RADIO

How can you communicate clearly by radio and across language barriers? The Canadian linguist Jean-Paul Vinay tried to answer this question. In 1949, he came up with a special alphabet. Working with the International Civil Aviation Organization (ICAO), he found words—one for each letter and number—that are easy to understand in English, Spanish, and French. These words were also selected because they are easy to pronounce for pilots all over the world and have no negative associations. The system prevents confusion between different letters and numbers.

There was a similar alphabet before the Second World War, known as the Able Baker alphabet, but that one was designed with only English speakers in mind. After the war, it no longer suited the increasingly international world of

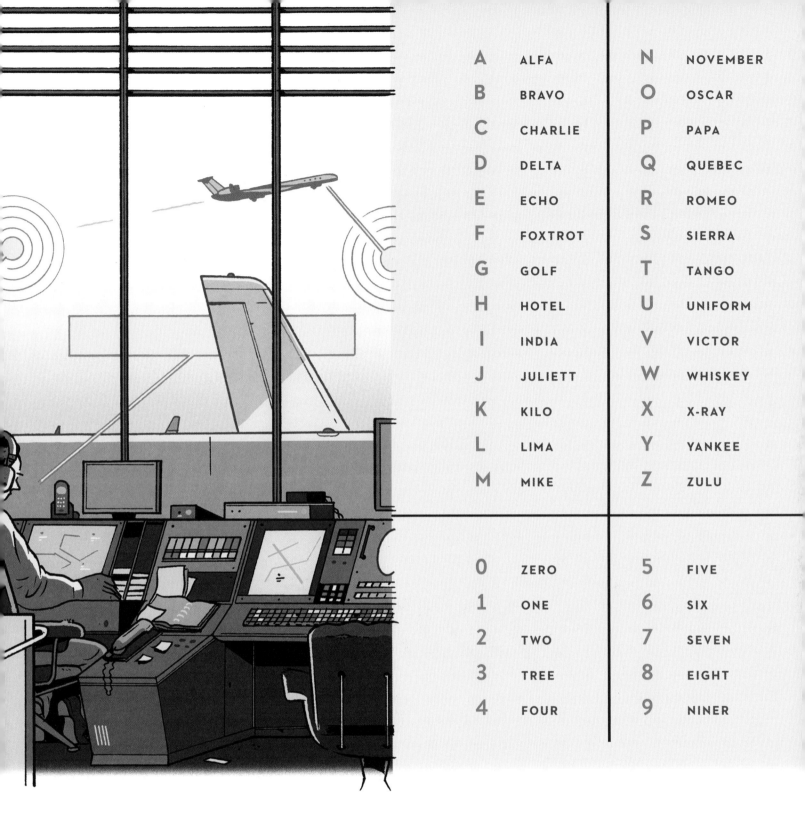

A	ALFA		N	NOVEMBER
B	BRAVO		O	OSCAR
C	CHARLIE		P	PAPA
D	DELTA		Q	QUEBEC
E	ECHO		R	ROMEO
F	FOXTROT		S	SIERRA
G	GOLF		T	TANGO
H	HOTEL		U	UNIFORM
I	INDIA		V	VICTOR
J	JULIETT		W	WHISKEY
K	KILO		X	X-RAY
L	LIMA		Y	YANKEE
M	MIKE		Z	ZULU

0	ZERO		5	FIVE
1	ONE		6	SIX
2	TWO		7	SEVEN
3	TREE		8	EIGHT
4	FOUR		9	NINER

aviation. Jean-Paul Vinay's alphabet was tested by air traffic controllers, pilots, and radio operators of thirty-one different nationalities. Since 1956, it has been in use worldwide. Pilots who need to spell things out can employ this method to avoid misunderstandings.

Every airplane is also equipped with a transponder. When an antenna on the ground releases a certain signal, the transponder responds automatically. It can also send out its own signal selected by the pilot. This signal is a four-digit code. The code for a hijacking is 7500, for radio failure, 7600, and for an emergency, 7700.

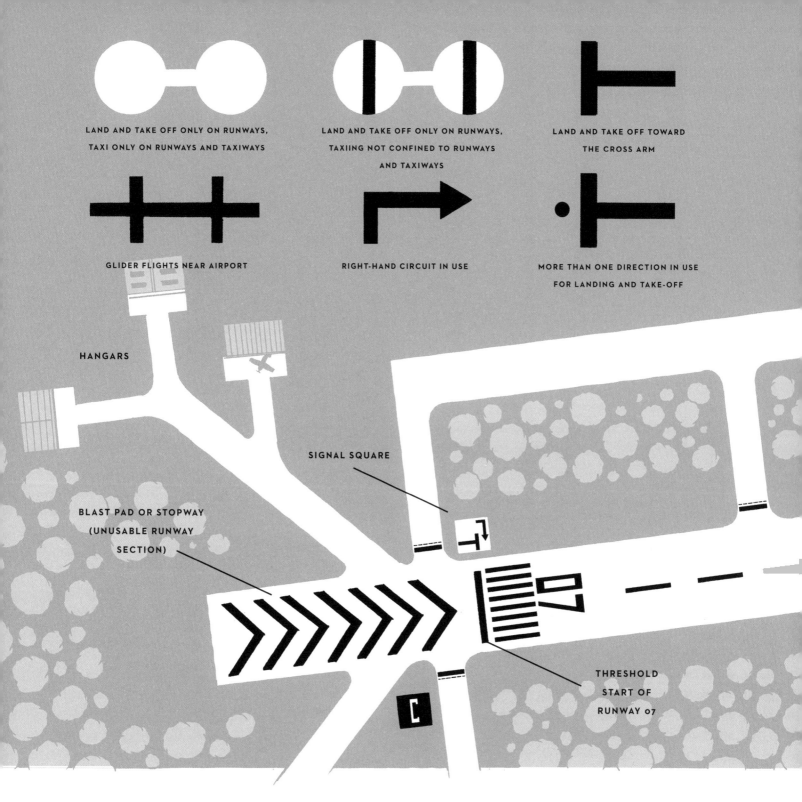

LAND AND TAKE OFF ONLY ON RUNWAYS,
TAXI ONLY ON RUNWAYS AND TAXIWAYS

LAND AND TAKE OFF ONLY ON RUNWAYS,
TAXIING NOT CONFINED TO RUNWAYS
AND TAXIWAYS

LAND AND TAKE OFF TOWARD
THE CROSS ARM

GLIDER FLIGHTS NEAR AIRPORT

RIGHT-HAND CIRCUIT IN USE

MORE THAN ONE DIRECTION IN USE
FOR LANDING AND TAKE-OFF

HANGARS

SIGNAL SQUARE

BLAST PAD OR STOPWAY
(UNUSABLE RUNWAY
SECTION)

THRESHOLD
START OF
RUNWAY 07

C

COMMUNICATION THROUGH SYMBOLS ON THE GROUND

The radio and transponders are not the pilot's only way of
receiving messages from the ground. Airports also have a
signal square, a small patch of ground containing symbols
clearly visible from the air. When pilots come in for a landing,
they first have to pass over the square and read the symbols.
Here, the signal field indicates that Runway 07 and the right-
hand circuit are in use.

There are also symbols on the airport runways and taxiways.
Broad strips across each runway show where the usable section starts and ends. These strips are known as thresholds.
The unusable section, or stopway, is marked with chevrons
(arrowhead symbols) up to the threshold. To reach the
runways, a departing airplane uses the taxiways. The aircraft
must always wait at the end of the taxiway, which is marked

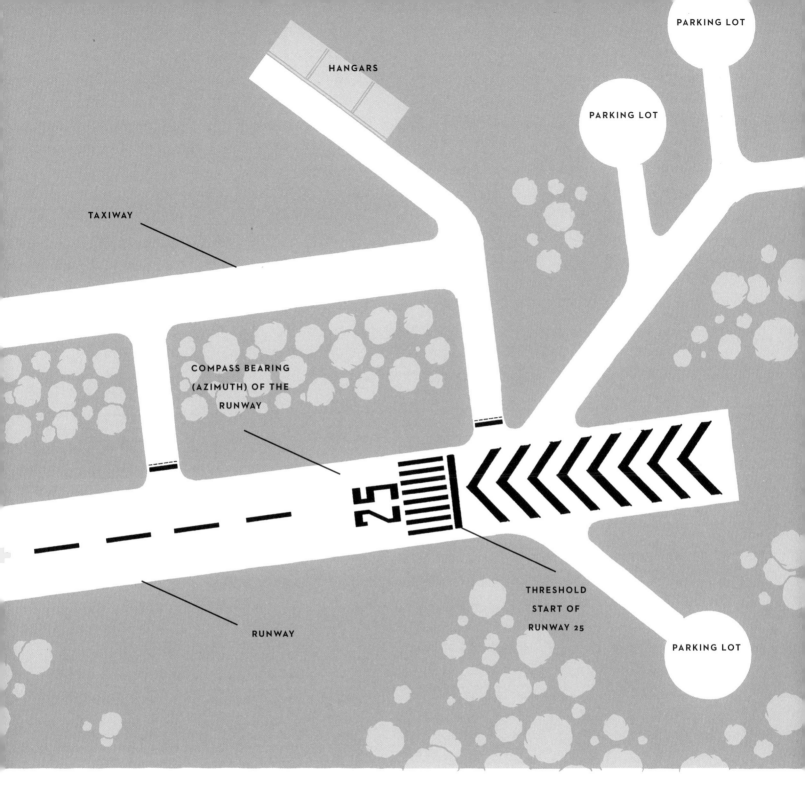

PARKING LOT

PARKING LOT

HANGARS

TAXIWAY

COMPASS BEARING
(AZIMUTH) OF THE
RUNWAY

25

THRESHOLD
START OF
RUNWAY 25

RUNWAY

PARKING LOT

with a broken line followed by a solid line.

The runway is also marked with a number according to its compass bearing—its angle relative to the Earth's magnetic north pole, divided by ten. In this illustration, you can see two airport runways, RWY 07 and RWY 25. RWY 07 is at a 70-degree angle relative to magnetic north, and RWY 25 is at a 250-degree angle. An airplane takes off against the wind,

so the runway with the strongest headwind will be used. Large airports often have a number of intersecting runways in various directions, so that one runway always has the best possible orientation to the wind.

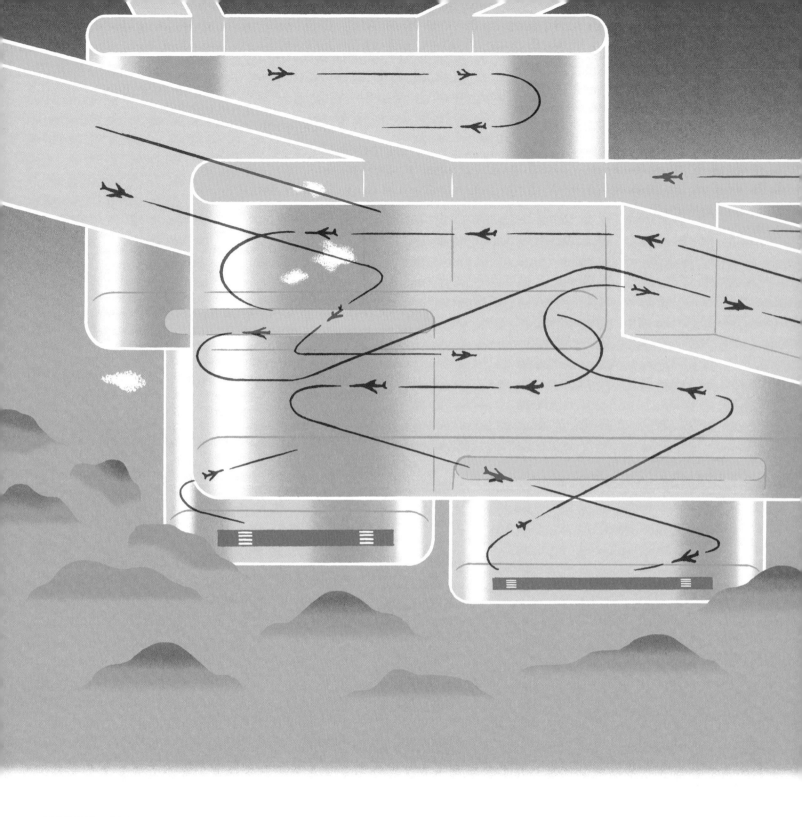

HOW IS AIRSPACE ORGANIZED?

Airplanes can't just fly through the air any way they choose. Around the world, airspace is organized by international agreements that keep air traffic safe. Airports, for instance, are hubs of air traffic, and every airport has an air traffic control service that manages incoming and outgoing flights. When an airplane enters the airspace of an airport, it is tracked by radar and an air traffic controller. The controller talks to the pilot and issues instructions, so that airplanes will maintain a safe distance from one another and the pilot won't land until a runway is available.

Long-haul international flights at high altitudes are the responsibility of a different group of air traffic controllers. They track routes called corridors or airways, which are like imaginary highways through airspace. But not every part of

the world has air traffic control. In some place, it is the pilot's job to watch out for other aircraft. When the airplane passes back into a control area, the pilot has to re-establish contact with the local air traffic control service. The pilot then has to fly in circles until receiving permission to enter the airspace. There are some areas over which aircraft are rarely or never allowed to fly. Besides this prohibited airspace, there are also restricted and danger areas. For example, no air traffic is permitted over the Houses of Parliament in London or the White House and U.S. Capitol in Washington, D.C., which means no airplanes are allowed to pass over those areas, even at high altitudes.

wind
165°

HOW DOES AN AIRPLANE NAVIGATE?

In heavy fog or during night flights, pilots cannot see land-marks. They then have to rely on their instruments to fly onward. Those instruments not only help them to control the airplane, but also to navigate to distant places. Nowadays, pilots can use Global Positioning System (GPS) equipment to figure out where they are headed. And if that doesn't work, there are also tower-like structures called radio beacons. A beacon sends out a signal on a special frequency that can be picked up by a radio on board the airplane. A device in the cockpit then indicates the heading that the pilot should follow.

Using a radio beacon is not always as straightforward as it sounds. Wind often pushes the craft off course, a phenom-enon called drift. If the pilot doesn't make allowances for

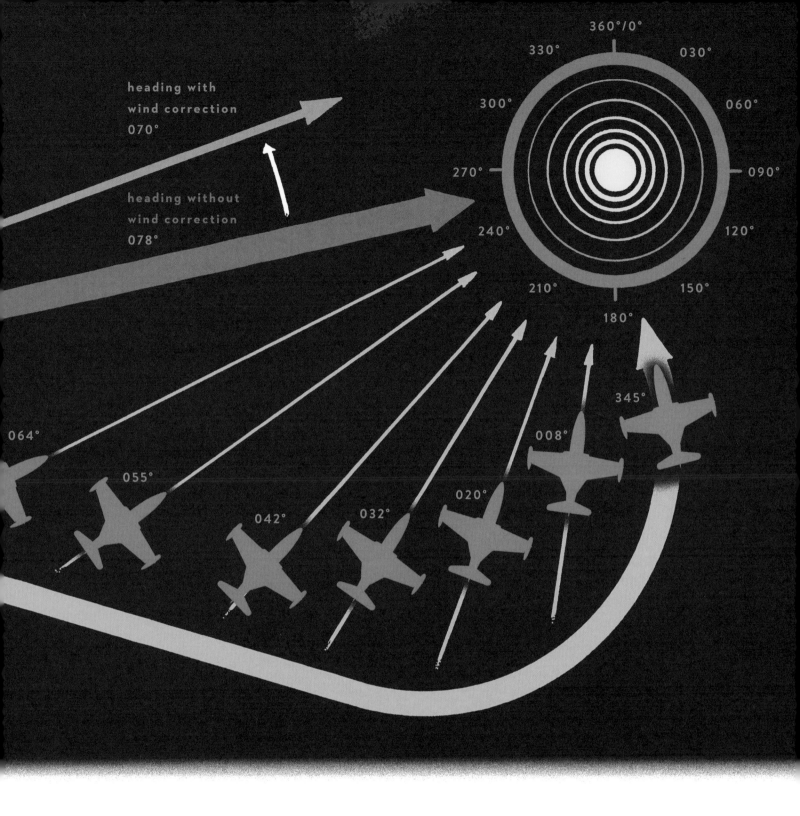

heading with
wind correction
070°

heading without
wind correction
078°

360°/0°
330°   030°
300°   060°
270°   090°
240°   120°
210°   150°
180°
345°
064°
055°
042°   032°   020°   008°

drift, the airplane will be blown farther and farther off course and have to change its heading to reach the beacon, taking extra time and extra fuel. This method is called homing, and it's the result of inexpert navigation.

To avoid the need for homing, a pilot preparing for a flight must calculate the drift correction required to negate the effect of the wind and fly straight toward the beacon. If this calculation is correct, the aircraft will fly with its nose always pointed toward the corrected heading, and it will follow the track straight to the beacon. That's called tracking, and it's the origin of the expression 'Right on track.'

THE FUTURE OF FLIGHT

DEVELOPMENTS IN AIRCRAFT TODAY

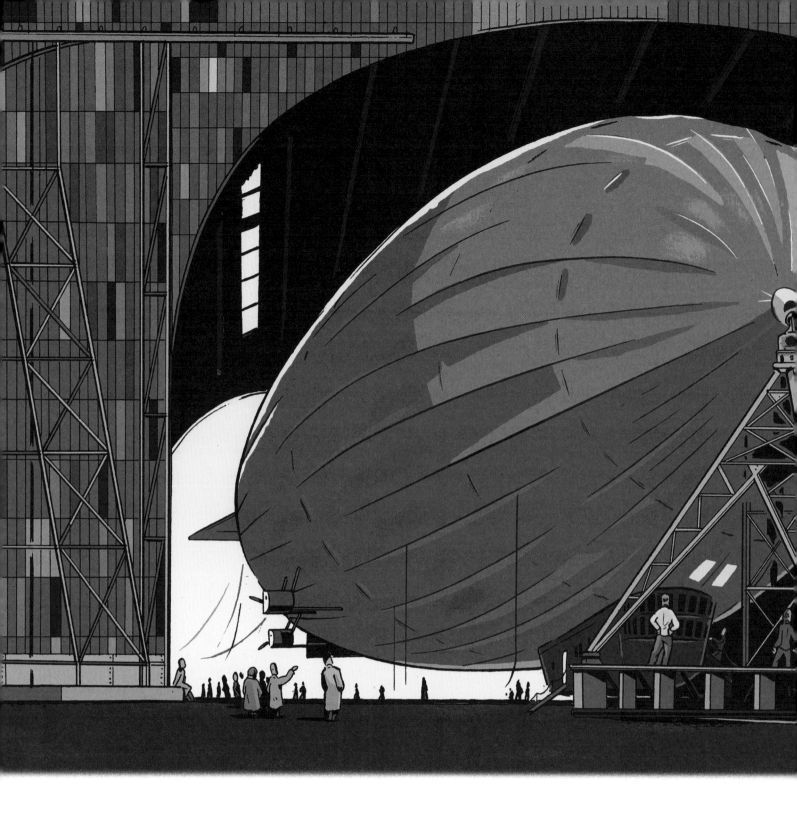

THE ZEPPELIN

The Zeppelin was among the most impressive sights to grace the skies during the early twentieth century. This large, cigar-shaped balloon with an aluminum frame was invented by Ferdinand von Zeppelin, a German count who invested a fortune in its development. Zeppelins got off to a rough start but gradually became more and more popular among the wealthy elite. That is, until 1937, when their fortunes changed.

When the LZ-128 Hindenburg tried to land at Lakehurst Naval Air Station, near New York, it burst into flames. Terrifying images of the disaster were seen around the world. All at once, the age of the Zeppelin was over.
But in 1993, Count Zeppelin's company resumed its activities in Friedrichshafen, the airship's birthplace. A new Zeppelin was developed called Zeppelin NT (New Technology).

The British aircraft manufacturer Hybrid Air Vehicles is also working on a craft that is lighter than air, thanks to a large volume of helium. The Airlander, known in full as the HAVE 304-Airlander 10, is quiet as a mouse and environmentally friendly. Its round, streamlined form has earned the airship its nickname, "the flying bum." In time, a model may be developed that can transport passengers in style, with sleeping cabins offering spectacular views through a glass floor. The Airlander may provide a much more appealing mode of travel than today's crowded airplanes. But Airlander passengers will need to have some extra time on their hands. The airship does not move fast—barely 150 kilometers per hour (93 mph)—and can remain aloft for up to five days.

THE FLYING CAR

The dream of making flying cars is almost as old as the automobile itself. As traffic jams have grown worse, this idea has popped up again and again. Even today, flying cars are still in the minds of engineers, although still far from becoming a reality.

Flying cars must meet many different criteria. They need to be practical, safe, and easy to drive. Ideally, a pilot's license should not be required. As long ago as 1926, Henry Ford had plans to produce a flying car, the Ford Flivver, but the project was shut down after an accident in which the pilot died. Since then, many experiments have been tested and abandoned. The flying car makes frequent appearances in movies, such as *Chitty Chitty Bang Bang, Back to the Future, Star Wars,* and *Blade Runner*. Moreover, now that drones, GPS systems,

TAYLOR AEROCAR N-101D / 1954

and self-driving cars have come into our lives, visionary entrepreneurs have returned to the flying car idea. In Silicon Valley, for instance, the Canadian aviation company Opener is working on BlackFly, a single-seater with eight propellers. The American aviation company LIFE is in the process of developing Hexa, an electrically powered drone with eighteen rotors. In China, a drone taxi is in development, called the Autonomous Aerial Vehicle (AAV).

Will the flying car concept ever really take off? The answer remains unclear. Many people still see a solo flight as a leap into the unknown. On top of that, there are already lots of car accidents. If we have to watch out for other vehicles both on the ground and in the skies, traffic could become scarier than ever!

THE SON OF CONCORDE / 1969

The Concorde was the first and only airliner to exceed the speed of sound, carrying passengers from Paris to New York in the record time of three and a half hours. Because of the time difference, the hour that Concorde passengers arrived in New York was actually earlier than the hour when they left Paris. This craft was the flagship model of the airplane manufacturers Aérospatiale and British Aerospace.

However, not everyone was enthusiastic.
The Concorde met with opposition because it made unwanted noise: a loud boom whenever it broke the sound barrier. There were also concerns about air pollution and safety risks. The first flight to New York was cancelled when the United States refused permission to land.
Moreover, because a ticket cost more than 10,000 euros

or dollars, the aircraft was used almost exclusively by celebrities and wealthy businesspeople. The so-called Concorde Club included such famous names as Elton John, Sean Connery, Paul McCartney, and Queen Elisabeth II. Margaret Thatcher even had a favorite seat, 4C, which was reserved for her whenever she flew the plane.

In 2000, a Concorde crashed in Gonesse, France, near Paris.

The Concorde era was over—at least for a while. The dream of a supersonic aircraft remains appealing. Airbus, Aeron, Boom, Lockheed Martin, and NASA are all working on the "Son of Concorde," designed to be quieter, faster, more affordable, and more fuel-efficient. Experts say the new Concorde will not be available until at least 2030.

SOURCES

Aeronautical Information Publication (AIP), Belgium, 2019

Decré, Bernard, Association La recherche de l'oiseau blanc, blog, 2019

Decré, Bernard, "Cold Case," in *Portland Monthly Magazine*, Portland, United States, 2013

Decré, Bernard and Vincent Mongaillard, L'Oiseau blanc, L'enquête vérité, Editions Arthaud, France, 2014

Karpels, L., Private Pilot License training, BAFA Ben Air Flight Academy, Antwerp, 2017

Pretor-Pinney, Gavin, *The Cloud Collector's Handbook*, Sceptre, United Kingdom, 2009

Reed, R. Dale, *Wingless Flight: The Lifting Body Story*, University Press of Kentucky, 2014

Saint-Exupéry, Antoine de, *The Little Prince*, Pan Macmillan, 2016

Springer, Anthony M., *Aerospace Design: Aircraft, Spacecraft and the Art of Modern Flight*, Merrell Publishers, 2003.

Tangye, Nigel, *Teach Yourself to Fly*, Teach Yourself, 2017

The ICAO spelling alphabet, Annex 10 to the Convention on International Civil Aviation, vol. II, 1955, sixth edition October 2001

Vanhoenacker, M., *Hoe land je een vliegtuig?*, Uitgeverij Unieboek | Het Spectrum, 2018

Vlaamse Zweefvlieg Academie (VZA), foundation course in gliding, Ravels, 1981.

www.nasa.gov/centers/dryden/history/pastprojects/Lifting/index, 2017

www.planeandpilotmag.com/article/piper-archer-50-years-and-counting, 2016

ACKNOWLEDGEMENTS

Many thanks to my parents, who allowed their sixteen-year-old son to take flying lessons, to Philippe Barbaix for the pleasant hours spent among the clouds and for reawakening a dormant flying bug, and to my Flight Instructor (FI) Daniël Poelman for his patience in the cockpit and for correcting errors in my manuscript.

BIOGRAPHY

Jan Van Der Veken has his own studio, Fabrica Grafica, where he creates illustrations in a retro futuristic style. His work has been displayed in countless exhibitions, published in newspapers and magazines, and used on posters. His first monograph was published in 2013 by Gestalten in Germany, and in 2016 he was awarded the Culture Prize of his home city of Ghent.

Prestel Publishing Ltd.
16–18 Berners Street
London W1T 3LN

Prestel Publishing
900 Broadway, Suite 603
New York, NY 10003

Library of Congress Control Number: 2020934693
A CIP catalogue record for this book is available from the British Library.

Translated from the Dutch language by David McKay

Project management: Melanie Schöni
Copyediting: Brad Finger
Technical copyediting: Martin Cambré
Production management and typesetting: Susanne Hermann

Prestel Publishing compensates the CO2 emissions produced from the making of this book by supporting a reforestation project in Brazil. Find further information on the project here:www.ClimatePartner.com/14044-1912-1001

This book was published with the support of Flanders Literature (flandersliterature.be).

Verlagsgruppe Random House FSC® N001967

Printed in Poland

ISBN 978-3-7913-7441-3
www.prestel.com